See It, Like It, Do It
Achieving Your Dreams

by
Michael and Manuela Noel

M&M Publishing

See It, Like It, Do It
Achieving Your Dreams
by Michael and Manuela Noel

Copyright 2018 Michael and Manuela Noel

ISBN: 978-1-9991280-0-5

All rights reserved. No portion of this book may be reproduced mechanically, electronically, or by any other means, including photocopying, without permission of the publisher or author except in the case of brief quotations embodied in critical articles and reviews. It is illegal to copy this book, post it to a website, or distribute it by any other means without permission from the publisher or author.

Limits of Liability and Disclaimer of Warranty
The author and publisher shall not be liable for your misuse of the enclosed material. This book is strictly for informational and educational purposes only.

Warning – Disclaimer
The purpose of this book is to educate and entertain. The author and/or publisher do not guarantee that anyone following these techniques, suggestions, tips, ideas, or strategies will become successful. The author and/or publisher shall have neither liability nor responsibility to anyone with respect to any loss or damage caused, or alleged to be caused, directly or indirectly by the information contained in this book.

Publisher
M&M Publishing
Coquitlam, BC
Canada

Printed in Canada and the United States of America

For Additional Copies visit:
www.seeitlikeitdoit.com

Table of Contents

Reader Reviews	vii
Dedication	ix
Special Thanks	xi
Foreword	xiii
Introduction	xv

Chapter 1: Hi, Honey, I'm Home!	**1**
Seizing the Unknown Challenges	4
Flying East for a Life Unknown	5
Starting Over	5
Learning Life's Lessons Very Young	6
When Fate Lends a Hand	8
A Test of Love	9
Dancing Through Life	10

Chapter 2: The World's Our Oyster	**13**
Except for Bungee-Jumping	15
Following Beauty	17
Jack of All Trades, Master of the World	19
Look to the Community	21
Comfort Zones Versus Adventures	23

Chapter 3: Loving Life as a Serial Entrepreneur	**27**
First Things First!	29
Boy, Were We Naive	30
The Right Staff	32
Make Things Happen by Listening to Your Gut	33
Give Up Your Day Job?	35
Don't let Opportunity Pass You By	38
Bottom Line	39

Chapter 4: The Kiss That Changed Our World — 41
What's in a Name? — 43
Our Mission — 44
Re-inventing Our Freedom — 45
So How Do We Help Others? — 47

Chapter 5: Living by Example — 51
The Jennifer and Dale Story — 53
And the Story Continues — 58
Not All Stories Have a Happy Ending — 60
Rent-To-Own Background — 62

Chapter 6: Life Waits for No One — 63
What Makes Us Stronger — 65
Changing Gears — 67
Live in the Now — 69
Life Is What You Make It — 70
Make Every Day Count — 71
Kidnapping Out of Town Visitors — 72

Chapter 7: Happiness Starts at Home — 75
Home Sweet Home — 77
Taking It a Step Further — 80
Any Dream Is Possible — 83

Chapter 8: Living Life to the Fullest — 85
Life, On Your Own Terms — 87
Achieving Their Dream, by Jennifer and Dale — 88
Food for Thought — 93
The Left Turn Syndrome — 94
Let Your Hair Down — 96
Smarter Spending — 97

Chapter 9: Do it Right, the First Time Around!   **101**
Fighting with Alligators?   104
Watching out for Your Backsides   105
Your Net Worth Equals Your Network   110

Chapter 10: It's The Memories That Count   **113**
Finding What Works in Life   115
And the Fun Is Just Beginning   117
What's More Fun Than a Barrel of Monkeys?   118
Life Has Its Rewards   119
Waste Not   122
Pay It Forward   124

Reader Reviews

In *The Kiss That Changed Our World*, Mike and Manuela tell the inspiring story of two very different people, through their shared sense of adventure. They keep their relationship fresh, and seize the excitement and passion that are life, by leaving their comfort zone. From their different upbringings, to a chance late night coffee date, their lives came together forever.

Alan Kane, MD,
FACSn, California

Love blossoms in the strangest places. Even what may seem like an intruder in *Honey, I'm Home*, turns out to tempt fate, twisting it into escapades of flying to Paris for dinner, collecting wine, and even a kissing a camel in Petra. Mike and Manuela are living life by the seat of their pants, from what appears to have all started with taking risks.

Douglas Adkins
Retired Engineer, Washington

WOW! I want to dance in their playground. Life on the edge is appealing, and we love where risks can take you, from the exotic corners of the world, to our own backyard. It was refreshing to read a story that takes you in the directions of possibilities, where you may have never thought before to be real, other than in a dream.

Kecia Doke
Writer, Colorado

See It, Like It, Do It

This was a fun read for me. I am a senior citizen who has lived a full, extraordinary life, but stayed home to raise six children. Although life was very fulfilling for me, there were times I would daydream of travel and crazy adventures. Reading about the journeys that Mike and Manuela experienced was almost as though I had been there. Now, I have had the best of two worlds!

Vonnie Sanders
Retired, Montana

Manuela and Mike have created a masterpiece that should be read by everyone who desires a jolt of motivation and inspiration. From their mutual humble backgrounds, to their amazing achievements, they will walk you through their ups and downs, and share their wisdom on how to live life to the fullest. Their first encounter is hilarious, and they personify the belief that spontaneity and synchronicity are an important part of a life well lived.

I highly recommend this book for its simplicity and time honored principles that are sometimes lacking in today's world. It will definitely inspire you to live your best life!!

Roy Prevost
Turbocharge Your Retail Business – How to Outmaneuver and Outperform the Big Guys

To know Mike and Manuela is to know love. A love that goes beyond the romantic sense of what a husband and wife can share. Together, their love for pursuing a truly fulfilled life by design—where they stay true to their hearts' desires, make all their own decisions, and embrace the challenges that come with them—is what fuels the notion where learning is the reward. I'm honoured to have witnessed firsthand the magic these two can create. As enthused collectors of life experiences and lessons, there is no doubt that this book has something to offer everyone.

Tim Tsai
Mentor

Dedication

Dedicated to our parents, Joyce and Emile Noel (who departed my life much too early), and Anita and Albino Giacomini, without whom this book and experience would not be possible.

Their love for teaching us about enjoying life, taking responsibility, and giving back to others, we are forever grateful.

Special Thanks

To Jennifer Smith and Dale Gangloff for their commitment to each other, and for setting an example for others to follow. We are truly proud of them and their accomplishments. Working with people like Jennifer and Dale makes it all worthwhile for us, not to mention gaining a new lifetime friendship.

To Rosemary *"Mamie"* Adkins for her inspiration and guidance, not to mention re-energizing us to complete this book. She is an amazing person, being very knowledgeable and fun to work with. Without Mamie's support, we would not have been able to finish this book.

To all of our readers, we thank you for your support and wish you a successful journey in life, taking one step at a time, never giving up your dreams, and reaching for the sky. Remember, your life's possibilities are only limited by your imagination and what you do yourself.

Foreword

Have you ever wished your life could be different ... or looked at your friend's or neighbor's life and wondered how your world could be like theirs? Well, life may throw many different challenges at you, but how you deal with them is of your own doing. Authors Mike and Manuela Noel have masterfully written and shared with you the journeys they have taken to find their dreams and make them a reality.

This awe-inspiring and sensational book, *See It, Like It, Do It*, leaves you with no doubt that you too, can make every dream happen, if only you never give up on your vision and determination for success.

Through example, they have shared one experience after another, including the good and the bad times, in order to show you that working hard with determination is what you need to succeed. Mike and Manuela are not magical people who waved a wand or twitched their nose; they are hard-working people who could see their dream, kept it in sight, and did whatever was necessary to make it a reality.

Mike and Manuela Noel will show you how to turn what was a dream into a reality. Why just look at your dream through the clouds? If you find yourself wishing for more…that is okay, but take action and do not expect it to come without effort, or for someone to hand it to you. Stretch until your reach goes no further, and then push a lot harder.

Do you have a desire to look your dream straight into the core and make it become a reality? My advice to you, read this book and learn how the other half lives and see how you too, can make it happen! Visit their web site for additional inspiration you may need at: www.SeeitLikeitDoIt.com

Raymond Aaron
New York Times Bestselling Author

Introduction

Sometime back, Mike and I came together with our minds and hearts, discovering what we both wanted in life. It was not long before we realized everything was the same, and it boils down to this:

- In our lives, *Life* has been our teacher.
- Our minds have been the highways.
- So then, *Learning* was the reward.

Life's a teacher. A mind is the highway. Learning is the reward. With these words echoing in our minds, we decided it was time to begin sharing our plans with each other, rather than to sit idly by dreaming…and simply plan on how we *were going to do what we wanted in life, rather than to just sit and dream or plan them alone in our minds.*

After all, if *life is a teacher*, hopefully, we had been paying attention; if the *mind is the highway*, only your own thoughts and imagination can limit your plans; and, certainly, if *learning is the reward*, we would not want to stifle our learning process! This made perfect sense as the starting place for our journey!

Mike and I decided we would rather think up, execute, and fail at something crazy than not to have done anything at all. So get up, follow your dreams, work hard, practice at your landings, and then go for it! You will persevere, if you make sure your plan is solid and the heart is sincere. You must either find a way to accomplish your dreams of a better life or make your own way. Either way, expect a few bumps along the way, but do not ever give up! Remember, if you play in a little pond, you will always be little, so set your sites on the lakes and rivers, and your dreams will soar, taking one step at a time, putting one foot in front of the other, but always moving forward. Set those sights high, with *higher* being even better. Now, expect the most incredible dreams to become a reality, but do not believe they will be *someday*, but *know* they will happen *now, if you do not allow anyone, especially yourself to stand in your way*!

No matter how hard you wish for it—with your hand over your heart and your eyes shut tight—life doesn't always serve up what you want. However, if you stay open and trust that *Life* is on your side, it will dish up more fun and adventure than you could have hoped for, but in the most unexpected forms and places.

For me, Michael, my adventure began with these four little words: *"Hi Honey, I'm home!"*

These are words that can be heard in households around the world on any given day. When I first said them, however, it was on a night that was far from typical, and I had never previously met Manuela, the woman to whom I uttered those fond words. At that time, she was just a dark shape huddled under blankets on a bed. That didn't put me off, however, and I quickly added, "Let's go for coffee."

For me, Manuela, when I heard this strange man say those words to me in my darkened bedroom, I admit I was a little unsettled at first. However, with my eyes shut tight, in half-sleep, and with only a moment's hesitation, I replied, "Yes." I had made it my policy to always say yes to life, and just like that, with one word, I met Michael. He is now my husband, my best travel companion, my ballroom dancing partner, my business partner, and my soulmate of 30 years—I'm so glad that I chose to say yes on that fateful night!

It was 3 o'clock in the morning, and I had just finished a long, tedious night shift at the gas station. As a recent immigrant to Canada from Switzerland, I was working long hours at whatever jobs I could get. I studied English in night school, and worked day and night to ensure that my dream of living here permanently would come true. I deeply desired to live in Canada, and I knew I had to do everything possible to make it work.

I started out as a nanny to a family, quitting my job as a media consultant in Switzerland for the chance to come here. When Michael stepped into my life, I was clocking long hours; I cared for children during the day, then worked from 6pm to 1am at a gas station, weekdays and most weekends, and from 4am to 8am at a bakery, Monday to Friday. I could have ignored that strange male voice saying *"Hi honey, I'm home,"* and gone back to sleep, and perhaps chosen to believe that it was just a dream. By that time, however, I'd learned that life really rewards you when you seize

Introduction

the opportunities it presents, so I knew I had to say *yes.*

Since that day, Mike and I have flown from Vancouver to Paris, enjoyed the finest of dinners, to then return home. We've also toured the best vineyards in British Columbia, Napa Valley, France, and New Zealand, coming away with hundreds of cases of wine to enjoy later as memories of our times together. I've even kissed a camel in Petra, while Mike has driven a tank over a car in New Zealand! How's that for added adventure and excitement? These and many other journeys can be yours too, if only you have a plan in life and are willing to work hard.

We had recently roamed in the wild, with graceful giraffes and African lions that we were so close to that we could have actually reached out and touched them. As a treat for ourselves, we experienced an expertly performed massage, on the white sands of Zanzibar.

We were also off on another escapade to Antarctica, where we played with penguins. We still have on our bucket list more that we want to ensue, which includes: flying a fighter jet, going to the Arctic to observe polar bears, playing in the best playground *ever*—the whole, wide world—while we continue to support our community.

Adventures await each of us, and we're thrilled to share ours with you. We do so not to make you envious of us or to boast of our wealth, but to spur you to live this precious life you've been given, to the max, because we want you to spend the days you have left in fun, exciting, and awesome ways. We want to see you stand before vistas that leave you breathless, and to witness wild animals prowling the plains as they did before man first stood on two feet. We encourage you to scale snow-capped mountains and listen to the harmonious and resonant chanting of monks in saffron robes. We want you to fall in love with the world, and with your life. If canoeing down a quiet river is what grabs you, then we want to see you go for it. What matters is that you find your passion and start working towards it, today.

Here is some food for thought: fifty years is only 18,250 days. You can't get a single one of those days back once they're gone, but you can make the best of the days you have remaining. Not irresponsibly, mind you; we don't recommend that you max out your credit cards and live in debt in order to check things off your bucket list. We know how important it is to live within your means, because we weren't born with silver spoons in our mouths, or even spare change. We just learned to budget and save for what we want, and to invest what money we have wisely. For Mike, being in debt is something to be avoided at all costs. He understands that taking on loan capital and mortgages is sometimes necessary, but he's always paid off his debts before they were due, in an effort to keep as much of his money as possible.

Don't think of *budget* as a dirty six-letter word. Rather, view it as a great tool to help you get what you want within a reasonable timeframe. What really matters is to set your sights on a goal, and then pull out all the stops to achieve it. Flying to Paris for one night just to have dinner at the magnificent Tour d'Argent restaurant may seem frivolous to some, but it was something we both really wanted to do. So, we planned, kept track of our airline points, and saved what we needed to make this dream a reality. It took us nine months to make it happen, but it was worth every penny and every moment spent putting the pieces in place, because the special memory we created for ourselves there is irreplaceable. Achieving this dream also helped us prove to ourselves, once again, that we can do anything we put our minds to—where there's a will, there is always a way!

We encourage you to dream big, live bigger, and do what you love, without hesitation or reservation. We share our experiences and lessons learned here in the hope you may find some inspiration for action towards your own dreams and goals. We, Michael and Manuela, are two people living extraordinary lives, because we've anchored ourselves in the belief that the world is extraordinary, and it is there for our enjoyment. When the world inspires a dream in you, we encourage you to please not ignore it, but to do all you can to find a way to make it happen. Make a left turn somewhere, explore, and enjoy what life has to offer.

We invite you to join us on our journey through this book, and to gain the inspiration you need to live the life of your dreams. *"People often say that motivation doesn't last. Well, neither does bathing—that's why we recommend it daily." – Zig Ziglar*

Go forth and live a mind-bogglingly amazing life.

Manuela and Michael

Chapter 1
Hi, Honey, I'm Home!

Chapter 1
Hi, Honey, I'm Home!

> **Where we love is home - home that our feet may leave, but not our hearts.**
> Oliver Wendell Holmes, Sr.

You can travel a journey of a thousand miles, only to realize that everything you could ever want or need had always been waiting for you at home. You can live a hundred years and never stop discovering new and fascinating things about the place you call home. *What is a home, anyway? What does that word mean to you?*

For us, home is so much more than just a house full of furniture, curtains, and clothes. For us, home is a work of art that we have created together, a labor of love established by two artists perfectly attuned with each other. After all, what do a Swiss vintner's daughter and a Canadian bank teller's son have in common? We came from different corners of the globe, and from very different life experiences. However, behind the superficial differences between us, is a common vision that has led us to build the life we now share together.

A home doesn't have to be a mansion, with many rooms and a garage full of luxury vehicles. A home can be a one-story bungalow, a two-story townhouse, or even a studio apartment. To us, the concept of home is much bigger than just a roof over our heads, a door, and a few windows. It's the comfortable sofa that is long overdue for a trip to the upholsterers, or the dented kitchen pots in which many warm meals have been cooked, and the emotions shared with each other. It's that recycled dining room table that was rescued from the dumpster, polished and shined so that it looks new again. Home is where the memories of side-splitting laughter with family and good friends happen over a meal; the happy thump-thump-thump sound of our dog's tail; it's also the dirty laundry and clothes that are stained and dusty from working in our garden, because we are living life to the hilt. And it's also the garden that bursts with riotous colors in the spring, providing us with the backdrop for where dreams are planned.

Seizing the Unknown Challenges

Neither of us have ever looked at a challenge and said, *"No thanks; that looks too hard."* More than anything, this willingness of ours to take on life by its terms, binds us together and has allowed us to create a home that has withstood the test of time. Where hard times and intelligence fall short, there's always compassion, for each other and the things we love most in life!

Life always has its ups and downs, and to that, we both say, *"That's what makes it interesting."*

To us, a great life is one that brings surprises at every turn and is full of challenges. It's all about how you meet those challenges that tax your patience, and how you use them to grow into the best version of yourself. For both of us, those challenges began early in life. Let us show you how we faced our trials …how we welcomed those grand openings and opportunities that just took our breath away, and how we learned that very often, life gives you a helping hand, when you least expect it.

Flying East for a Life Unknown

My childhood, as the daughter of a Swiss vintner was idyllic in some ways. Our family was far from rich, but my parents were wise people who had a tight hand on the budget and kept everyone happy and well-fed. Food is central to my favorite childhood memories; my mother made everything from scratch, with the freshest ingredients, and kept the house warm with the delicious aromas of simple, mouth-watering home cooking.

Early on, I noticed that inexplicably, our home would receive many visitors around lunchtime. This was no coincidence as it turned out; people in the region knew what a good cook my mother was, and they also knew that no one would be turned away without a meal. Sometimes there were as many 15 hungry people around the table, and this taught me that food is community. Food adds texture and taste to life, and to this day, Mike and I continue to open our kitchen to friends, family, and strangers who drop in, without notice, for a bit of love and nourishment.

As the youngest of three children, and the only girl, I had to grow up fast. I quickly learned that I had to fight to get my needs met and earn my brothers' respect. That lesson hit home even harder when I lost my father at the tender age of 16, and then my mother, just six years later, at my age of 22.

After my mother died, I decided that it was time to leave Switzerland and create new memories in a new homeland. I set my sights on Canada, knowing that living there would give me an excellent opportunity to learn English. Have you ever let your heart lead you in a totally unexpected direction? For me, the courage to do this is what has allowed me to create the life of my dreams.

Starting Over

I knew when I left the country of my birth that I was never going to return. But little did I know, when I boarded the plane, this decision would open me up to so much of life, and that life would unfold so fully in response. All it takes is the courage to leave the familiar behind and to trust that life is grand, and that is exactly what I did.

Have you ever made a choice to leave like this, either emotionally or physically? If so, did you feel you would ever return?

I flew halfway across the world to Canada, determined to start my life anew. Before leaving, I had to secure a position as a nanny, since it was the only occupation allowed under the temporary work permit. As my young charge watched Sesame Street, I watched with her, hanging on every word as I taught myself English. I sounded out the foreign words, over and over again, not caring what I read as long as it taught me new words to add to my growing vocabulary.

After two years, I had gained immigrant status in Canada, which gave me the right to seek employment in any field I cared to work in. So it was that, in addition to caring for children, I took on morning shifts at a bakery, and late night shifts at a gas station, learning more and more about my adopted homeland in the process.

Money was tight in those days, and once in a while, I felt a pang of envy towards my carefree roommate, who had a very *play today, work tomorrow* mentality. After all, I was still very young, and such a carefree lifestyle appealed to me. However, having been raised by parents who got every bit of value out of their money, taught me that credit was to be avoided as much as possible, so even when my roommate tried to entice me out for nights on the town, I always ducked out, keeping my nose to the grindstone and working as hard as I could. I knew this would serve me well in the future, and it has.

There were times when I wondered about the fun opportunities that I was missing out on, but then one night, around 3 AM, opportunity came looking for me. While other women might have been terrified or angry at the form this particular opportunity came in, I chose to embrace it, and the rest is history!

Learning Life's Lessons Very Young

Where Manuela's upbringing was in some ways very traditional, mine was a little less stable. I was born in the mid 50's, to Canadian parents who were both in the Royal Canadian Air Force, stationed in France. However, when I wasn't even a year old, and my mother was pregnant with my brother, my father was killed in a routine fighter jet training mission.

After this traumatic event, Mom moved our small family back to London, Ontario, where she had family. Though life was far from easy for a mother on her own with two small boys in the 1950s, she managed to make ends meet. After working years as a bank teller, she had finally saved enough money for a down payment and mortgage on a small home, so with her desire to have a stable environment for her sons, she decided to buy her own home. However, back in those days, obtaining a mortgage for a single mom was no easy task, to say the least! I'm delighted to say, we were able to work it out. The mark of lean times stayed with her, however, and she always took care to make sure that her children understood where money came from.

My brother and I received money for doing chores, and Mom made sure to teach us how to spend only what we had, so if we didn't have the cash, it would have to wait until we did. Spending within our means, and learning to save for what we really needed, was always a priority. Buying on credit was viewed with suspicion, and we were taught to avoid it unless it was absolutely necessary to build up credit and buying power in later years.

Some people might have emerged from this early life experience with a rather insular worldview, and this was certainly true for some of my schoolmates. They never moved from their home town, and everything they've seen of foreign lands, they've seen through the television screen. They just never imagined there could be much more to the world beyond what they saw every day.

Who wants to live like that? Not me, and I'm guessing, not you, if you're reading this book!

I always hungered for something different, so I leveraged the skills I'd picked up as a young boy to take me to faraway places. I've been very mechanically inclined since the age of 10, when I would take apart radios and put them back together again, and I let that aptitude lead me to a career in computers.

Though money was always a concern, I chose to look for an opportunity where others might have perceived it lacking. I signed up for the Royal Canadian Naval Volunteer Reserve, and for seven years, I got amazing training in both mechanical and mental disciplines there. They paid me to see the world, and I took maximum advantage of it.

Of course, it wasn't all high times abroad. After the RCNVR, my next job was working as a produce clerk in a large grocery store. I combined that with another job in a beer store, in order to help make ends meet while I was in college. It was during that time spent bagging groceries and bottles of beer, and chatting with the diverse array of customers who walked into the store day and night, that I gained a great insight, which has served me well ever since: I realized that good customer relationships are essential, regardless of the business you're in. They are the fuel that lubricates the wheels of sales, and builds loyalty, which in turn, build on each other. I realized that no matter which side of the counter you're on, you should always be treated with respect, and this insight now permeates everything I do.

Life will take you to all sorts of interesting places if you are willing to sample all it has to offer without hesitation. That said, however, the most important events in your life can happen right in your backyard! Though my travels had taken me all over the world, I had no idea that I would find the one adventure that would do the most to catapult me into a lifetime of fulfillment, waiting for me in a bed in Canada, exhausted after her night shift, and completely unaware of my existence! That's when things really started to get good, and I'm so grateful for every moment we've shared since.

When Fate Lends a Hand

Fear and panic turns to love...Imagine this!

A young woman has just stumbled home after her late-night shift at a gas station. Before that, she had spent the whole day looking after children. The children are a delight, but being children, they had run her ragged before she even got to her night shift.

Now she is snug under the covers, relishing a rare chance to sleep in. On weekdays, she only has time for a few hours of sleep before she has to be at the bakery, but now it's the weekend and she can finally get some rest.

As it turned out, Manuela's roommate had gotten drunk, as she often did on the weekends. This time, however, instead of being dropped on the doorstep, where she would call through the mail slot for Manuela to come let her in (this happened so many times that Manuela stopped locking the door before going to bed), she had been driven home by Mike, who had decided that a drunk girl should not be sent home to fend for herself.

Suddenly, her peaceful rest is disturbed by the sound of an unfamiliar male voice calling out, *"Hi honey, I'm home! Put your pants on, and let's go for coffee!"*

Given the fact that the only other inhabitant of the house was supposed to be her female roommate, Manuela's abrupt response was only to be:

"It's 3 o'clock in the morning; who the hell are you?"

"I'm Mike, and I want to take you out for coffee!"

It was at that moment that fate intervened. Instead of being angry or upset, Manuela simply nodded drowsily and said that she would be right down.

That morning, Mike and Manuela talked until dawn at an all-night diner, and somewhere along the line, they realized that they could go on talking for the rest of their lives together.

A Test of Love

You don't get to pick your beginnings, but we wouldn't have ours any other way. It was brash, it was unexpected, and it proved that sometimes love comes calling when you least expect it.

In the days before cell phones, Mike and I didn't exchange telephone numbers. Instead, Mike took my number, and for the next week, I waited to see if he would call. The silent phone taunted me. However, just as I was just about to give up hope, I realized something.

Going through my home, I realized that every phone in the house had its ringer turned off! My roommate had wanted to get some sleep, so she had turned the ringers off on all the phones in the house to ensure she wouldn't be disturbed. We could make outgoing calls, but any incoming calls would be missed. This wasn't caught until the following Friday. In those days, answering machines were just coming on the market, and that was an expense we hadn't even considered taking on at that point.

My heart sank, and I grew very angry at my roommate at the idea of missing out on what could have been the love of a lifetime, but also at missed work opportunities as I was a court interpreter on call. Still feeling angry, I turned all the ringers back on.

You know, however, that the story does not end here. That very day, right after turning the ringers back on, the phone rang, and wonder of wonders, it was Mike…he had been trying to call all week, and was making his final attempt before giving up! So many things could have kept us apart, and reason would say that we should never have even met in the first place. Instead, from that strange meeting at 3 AM, and thanks to a drunken roommate, a marriage of 30 years has blossomed.

Dancing Through Life

Our life together has been built on many interests we share together, one of which is ballroom dancing. The excitement of each new step, as we glide along the floor, in sync with one another, balances our connection, both physically and emotionally.

Shall We Dance?

A while back, we added dance classes to our relationship to further enhance our partnership, and for the sheer joy of learning another activity together, as we believe that fun, with a little or a lot of standing on the edge, ignites a fire between the bonds of two people. Sensuous love of romance, music, and going out dancing adds that special spark of enthusiasm seen from the eyes of one another!

We all want a well matched and harmonious relationship, enjoying the moment with our partner, engulfed in passion for life. So, in addition, dance helps us, as partners, to reach our goal of constantly improving our expression of life.

While we were taking dance lessons, we had the opportunity to participate in a dance competition. It was not so much about winning the competition, but rather we thought it would be a lot of fun practicing and perfecting our moves. We practiced day and night, putting in countless hours all the time, and seeing the progress we made. This was our first competition, and while we did not expect to win, we placed first for the Jive, in our classification. Wow, it just goes to show you that when you put your mind to it, you can accomplish anything you want.

Dancing, to us, is like a fine balance of trusting each other through the ups and downs of life, and knowing when to take those leaps into the unknown.

Somehow, we knew that a 3 AM fateful meeting, while most people were sleeping, would be the beginning for the two of us, to fall in love, moving in perfect harmony over the next few decades, and stepping in time together, for all of eternity.

Chapter 2
The World's Our Oyster

I love you too Andre but a fish that big, really, I have never heard such a tall fish story before.

Chapter 2
The World's Our Oyster

Except for Bungee-Jumping

"We keep moving forward, opening new doors, and doing new things, because we're curious, and curiosity keeps leading us down new paths."
– Walt Disney

The thought of separating my ankles from the rest of my body somehow does not appeal to me, but there are thousands of people that think that is just fine. Whatever your passion, just do it…

Mike, **celebrating in New Zealand, driving a tank! Ooopppsss, ran over a car!**

Mike has driven a tank over a car in New Zealand, and Manuela has kissed a camel in Petra. Our marriage is fueled by our passion for each other and for life. After all, passion is what life is all about, and it is both the fuel you use to move forward and the reward for your efforts. To keep a marriage going, it's important to constantly add new things to it. We're not talking about new houses or faster cars (though we wouldn't say no to those things!) Instead, we're talking about new experiences that keep our relationship fresh, alive, and exciting.

Our adventures and experiences have left us with memories to last a lifetime, but the truth is that you do not need a fortune to live a diverse and exciting life.

In our home, you will likely find a cornucopia for viewing in every room! In other words, our life *runneth over* with the wealth that we each receive from one another with love, the excitement of living life, the joys of experiencing new adventures, impulsive excursions, and just whatever pleases our spur of the moment thoughts of pleasure! We live for life, and enjoy every minute in it. Live a lot, loving each new day. Wealth does not have to mean money. You can find activities that build your own inside wealth of happiness.

Here are a few ideas how you, too, can build your wealth of cornucopias for free or very little cost:

- The two of us enjoy the pleasure of exploring new wine tasting, and have discovered many wineries will offer free tours and a sample afterwards, in hopes of selling their wines.
- Build an inside fire, spread a blanket on the floor, and have a picnic right in the comfort of your own home.
- Have a giant bowl of popcorn and watch movies all night.
- Take an afternoon to treasure hunt garage sales…another man's junk may be your treasure!
- Prepare a special dinner and enjoy it by candlelight, catching up with each other's week, or simply have a romantic evening.
- Visit a car dealership for an expensive automobile, and take it for test drive!
- Pretend you are entertaining an out of town guest, and be a tourist in your own town.
- Go to a warehouse store that samples foods, and nibble your way through it.
- Get in your car after just waking, and drive to your friends' homes and pick them up for a *come as you are party*, and serve a *Make-Ahead Breakfast Casserole.*
- Go to the Humane Society and pet those lonely animals, abandoned, waiting for attention.
- Host a progressive dinner night with friends so it's little cost for each home, keeping it simple and ending with a dessert and board games, or reminisce about high school days.

In other words, let your hair down and enjoy life. It's time to *not* keep up with the Jones's but to love life and partake in every delicious bite!

Following Beauty

Manuela has never been a girl who had to have the best of everything, but she still loves beautiful things wherever she finds them. When she was setting up housekeeping as a young, single woman in Canada, she always made a point to stop at thrift stores and rummage sales, and set up her new kitchen with whatever pots and pans she found. Nothing matched, but that didn't change the taste of the food she made at all!

From her childhood in Switzerland, she learned that beauty and quality are not necessarily tied to price. Rather, she learned that there is beauty and a grace in functionality; that even if something is second hand, there is nothing wrong with this, as long as it serves its purpose. She's never seen the point in paying for a high-end designer purse, when the same amount of money could purchase ten purses that were just as lovely, even if they don't carry the label of a noted name in fashion.

Her favorite ways to express her aesthetic is with her jewelry, nail art, and sewing. She has loved jewelry ever since she was a child; she loves wearing it, and she loves all kinds of it. Of course, at a certain point, she realized that it's simply not possible to wear as much of it as she wants to! After all, one can't go out in public with canvases of art on one's nails, and with arms and neck dripping with rings and bracelets and necklaces, without attracting a few looks!

I've always said that tongues will be wagging wherever Manuela goes, and sure enough, it sometimes gets so loud, the gossip flies to the four winds! If I show up somewhere alone, and it's a place Manuela usually comes with me, I'm often asked, *"Where's Manuela, I want to see her nails!"* So much for wanting to see me.

Because she relishes collecting jewelry, and the pieces she buys are always dear to her, she decided to create a jewelry wall—a place where she could hang her pieces when they were not hanging from her. She arranged them carefully, grouping them so that when hung, they created a beautiful design on the bathroom wall.

Suddenly, a wall that had been plain and boring was decorated with flashes of metal and glass, imbuing the room with a gorgeous shine that would be difficult, if not impossible, to replicate with a purchased arrangement. The jewelry display is beautiful, but it also speaks volumes about the woman who created it. It says that she loves shine and sparkle, and that she delights in the various hues and shades of color and the texture of the stones. Some are glossy and smooth, some are rough and uneven, but they all tell a story of far-off or close-to-home places. Manuela also loves the act of creation, of stringing gems and findings of disparate weight and design into something eye-catching and beautiful. ***Her jewelry wall is a metaphor for her love of life.*** In the same manner as she wears her jewelry, Manuela cloaks herself with life experiences. Her jewelry reflects the wildness of an African safari, the classic elegance of a night in a Michelin three-star restaurant in Paris, the rough and tumble of a camel ride in the Jordanian desert, and of course, the comforts of the home we have built together.

Her creativity also extends to her love of wandering the aisles of a fabric store until the print of a fabric catches her attention. At that moment, she starts to visualize what it could look like once put together. She has created so many garments, five to ten years ahead of the fashion trend. A year ago, something caught her eye at a major hardware store; it was a safety lock used to put on doors for added security. Immediately, she knew that an amazing and unique jacket could be made with it, and she did just that. No other garment that she ever made got so much attention. Both men and women always ask her, *"Where on earth did you get that?"* Once, at a function we attended, a professional tailor, with a history of creating clothing for well-known designers, approached her to ask about the jacket. When she told him that she was both creator and designer of it, his jaw dropped and, once he got over the initial shock, he said, *"Those designers have nothing next to you."* She was very flattered and humbled by the compliment.

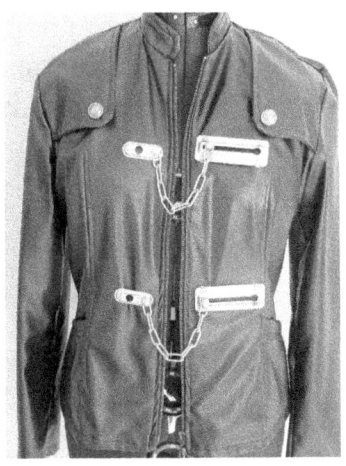

And of course, let's not forget her nails. They are a canvas that changes weekly. Often reflecting the season or holidays like Valentines' day, Halloween, or Christmas, they are also inspired by things Manuela encounters in the course of her everyday life.

Everyone always looks forward to seeing what unique creation her fingertips will be sporting each week, but this is only one of many ways that she pays homage to beauty in her life. She has taught me to appreciate the beauty in life as well, and it's one of the things I love most about her.

Jack of All Trades, Master of the World

Ever since I was a kid taking apart radios in my mother's small house, I've hungered to understand how things work. So much of my path has been shaped by looking at how the world works, and by exploring how I can shape it to my own benefit.

In my youth, I learned a little effort goes a long way, and I learned that if I just got off the couch and went after my goal, the world could change!

For example, when it comes to landscaping, I gave thought to how I could turn the land around the house into something that was more pleasing to the eye. Others would have called in the professionals, and still others would have decided that it was just too much trouble to mess with. They would have left the yard as dull as it looked before, but I have always marched to the beat of a different drummer.

I saw a solution, I figured out how to get it, and I went after it. Five years in the making, and a lot of Advil later, the result was a gorgeous backyard landscaped with two Koi ponds, 70 feet of meandering river, seven waterfalls, and 12,000 gallons of water. There were innumerable possibilities and countless decisions to make. Perhaps if I dug a little deeper here, I could get the water to rush and tumble on this stretch, and how do I get the water to eddy into the pond? Should this waterfall have a taller leap, and what about the other six? Many nights, I went to sleep to the imaginary sounds of bubbling water.

However, the day came when I could flick a switch, and a glorious symphony of gently flowing water and rushing currents filled our backyard. Together, Manuela and I had achieved something far more beautiful and far more impressive than a professional landscaper could have done for us. Just as importantly, the whole experience has made me something of an expert in how to design landscapes to get the desired look.

You can say the same thing about my love for cabinetry and woodworking. When it comes to putting cabinets together, most people will just leave it to the pros. However, I knew I wanted more than what's offered on the shelves of the hardware or furniture store—something unique—and I saw cabinet-making as one more skill I could acquire to help make our home more beautiful and functional.

The more I learned about woodworking and cabinetry, the more I realized that it would take some real work and concentration to do it well. But I felt confident I could handle it, and I embraced it wholeheartedly. There is something reassuring about running my hand over fine-grained wood grain, and something challenging about seeing finished shapes in a length of timber. Michelangelo's quote comes to mind: *"Every block of stone has a statue inside it, and it is the task of the sculptor to discover it."*

I have always viewed the world as an explorer's playground, rich with infinite possibilities, and Manuela shares this view. There is nothing that is too difficult or too much hassle to achieve once we put our minds to it. If someone else can make it, then why can't I? Some of my friends say that I take on too much, but it is the spirit of adventure, which I share with Manuela, that has given us success in business and a thriving life. We don't see problems or broken things; we only see possibilities and solutions.

Do you want to live a life of passion? You don't need to break the bank to do it. Neither Manuela nor I believe in buying on credit unless it helps to build up credit. Instead, make do with the money you have. Even if you are not bringing in that much money, you can still change the way you see the world. You can still go looking for experiences that will thrill you, enchant you, and bring you closer together with your special someone.

Look to the Community

One thing we both love is going on pub crawls together, on our bikes. We get to meet new people, have interesting and inexpensive drinks, and squeeze in some exercise and fresh air at the same time. Many people feel that when they go out, they need to dress to the hilt and spread a lot of cash around, but as far as we're concerned, that couldn't be further from the truth.

Before you run the risk of becoming melded to your couch, take a look at your local community calendar. Keep your mind open, and as you scan down the list, take note of any event that piques your interest. It might be an art crawl, where you get to visit the homes and studios of artists in the community, or it could be a hike in the woods or a snowshoeing adventure. You do not need to have any experience, just a willingness to roll up your sleeves and have fun!

Are you one of those people who second guesses yourself when the time comes to try something new? Why should you go to a free concert in the park, or why should you learn to play a new musical instrument? If it brings a smile to your face or fills you with satisfaction, then we say, *Why not?*

What is stopping you from having the time of your life? In most cases, when you get right down to it, the only thing that is holding you back is you. The only obstacle in your way is a mistaken belief that you do not have permission to have fun, and that you do not have the ability to get what you want.

We simply do not let thoughts like this stop us, and this *Why Not?* attitude has led to all sorts of amazing adventures. Some of these have kept us fairly close to home, while others have taken us across the globe. From driving a tank in New Zealand to a Kenyan safari, from a night out in Paris to a massage in Zanzibar, the world really is our oyster. Okay, we draw the line at bungee-jumping, but we know that a world of experience—sensory and sensual—waits for you as it has for us.

Think about the adventures you want, and remember that living an amazing life takes practice! If you are not yet ready to fling yourself out the door of a perfectly good airplane, with a parachute, then just start smaller. If you're a shy person, then maybe inviting some friends home to dinner would be an adventure for you. You may have two left feet and no sense of rhythm, and the thought of attending a ballroom dancing class makes you quiver. But we ask you—do you want to be remembered as a wallflower, or do you want to be known for having the courage to step out of your comfort zone to learn some smooth moves?

We're not suggesting that you live beyond your means—far from it! If you are willing to play within the bounds set by your budget, to save and to move forward when you can, you'll be paying it forward for even more experiences. Heading to Paris just for one night was done on a mix of thrifty frequent flyer miles and unexpectedly cheap fares. There are so many solutions available to you if you can just be open to them!

Comfort Zones Versus Adventures

Your comfort zone defines the limits within which you feel safe. You know every nook and corner of it, and this can be a wonderful thing when you are feeling stressed and afraid, because it gives you a place to reassess and regroup.

The issue is that everything you most want lies outside of your comfort zone. If you never leave its boundaries, you'll never venture very far from your front doorstep. If Mike hadn't had the courage to leave his comfort zone, he never would have left the town he grew up in. If I, Manuela, had never left my comfort zone, I would have stayed in Switzerland, to have never made it to Canada at all. We would have never met, and we most likely would have lived much different lives as a result.

Life is too short to waste on petty fears and doubts. Whenever something catches our eye, or an adventure intrigues us, we discuss it together, and then we usually run after it. If a possibility comes up, and you spend time debating whether you should pursue it or not, then in our opinion, you are wasting precious time having an argument with yourself, while life waits just outside your door. Many people think that time is money, but we know this is not true. Time is one of the most valuable things that you have, and once used, it can never be replaced. What you do with the time you have left is all that really matters. Personally, we would rather enjoy the time we have, and get the most out of life, without letting the *what ifs* and the *if onlys* of life hold us back.

Mike was always supportive and proud of what he felt were my artistic pursuits, to include jewelry, nails, and dressmaking, through which I would always be adding new pieces. He said they would just show up in time to add life and color to the whole of our world, at the perfect time. Mike had many passions in life as well, but cabinetry and landscaping were two he excelled with, especially when mastering new projects, which he uses to beautify our home and to keep it organized.

These passions that we pursue are not minor things. They are not things that you get good at on your first try. However, we are always looking to experience things that require an investment of time and passion, because we love the sense of accomplishment it gives us. It took Mike five years to landscape the backyard, and my jewelry and sewing are always a work in progress. It is not always easy following our passions and living an artistically engaging life. All we can tell you is that it beats the alternatives!

Many of you long to make a difference to the lives of others, but what are you doing to positively impact your own life? Are you ready to lead an interesting life? Do you want to live abroad? Start planning! You may have to tighten your budget and work two jobs for the next year or more. You may have to brush up on your language skills. But if you keep moving in the direction of your dreams, one day soon, you'll be posting Instagram pictures from Fiji, Australia, or your own, newly custom designed backyard. Here's to more adventures!

Comfort zones can become traps, and the way out of them is to push yourself. Sometimes you may need a nudge, just like a bird pushes her hatchlings out of the nest so that they spread their wings and fly. You need to be willing to let yourself grow and to allow yourself to take safe risks. Start small, and progress a little at a time. This is how you can nurture your passion for yourself, the world, and what is in it.

Do you realize that falling short in your life can usually be traced back to how you plan your goals and follow up with them? It is also the number one reason why individuals are not able to reach the lives they only envy from others.

Working on your own life is not easy, but to stay inside the comfort zones you have created for boundaries is by far the leading cause of life's disappointments. It's found that many feel it to be far easier to simply blame those that have the luxuries in life, than to look outside of the zone for what you need to change in order to reach your desired dreams for life.

Do you also realize that fear is why most people stay hiding inside of that comfort zone—the fear of the unknown or failure—and all because they were not prepared or willing to go the extra mile.

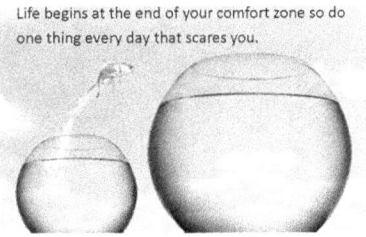

Why settle for less in life? Get up and out of your comfort zone, and dare life! You will be surprised at what you will find for yourself and loved ones.

Chapter 3
Loving Life as a Serial Entrepreneur

Chapter 3
Loving Life as a Serial Entrepreneur

Mike and I know that in life you'll never get ahead by waiting for something to happen—rather, you need to take action to make it happen. Early on in our marriage, we both knew that we wanted to own our own business. We knew that being entrepreneurs would give us the freedom and room for creativity that we wanted in our lives. Owning our own businesses did just that, but it also gave us an education in what works and what doesn't. While it wasn't originally our plan to become serial entrepreneurs, this is how it unfolded for us as we moved from one valuable learning experience to another. At each stage, we learned a little more about what we did and didn't want, which gave us the clarity to create the ventures that sustain us today.

Sure, it might have been easier if we had found exactly the right fit with our first business venture, but we have no regrets because we know that ultimately there are no mistakes, only learning opportunities. If you're attracted to the entrepreneurial lifestyle, there are no better things that will take you further than a commitment to learning as much as possible from every experience life brings to you. The most successful entrepreneurs have had multiple business ventures, some successful and some not so much. I feel that the journey Mike and I have traveled provides a valuable example of what this looks like in real life, and it's our sincere hope that reading about it here helps you find the courage to follow your heart.

First Things First!

In our quest to become business owners, Mike and I decided that the best way to grab that brass ring was to invest in a franchise, and we found one that we felt was perfect for us in the hair industry. It seemed like a great opportunity: the price to get into it was reasonable, the tools we would need were provided, and the royalties were a set fee instead of a percentage of our profits. We thought, *Wow! What a great opportunity!*

Boy, Were We Naive!

Although we had hoped it wouldn't come to this, it soon became clear that one of us would need to babysit our fledgling business, so Manuela quit her full-time job to plunge headfirst into an industry we knew next to nothing about. Of course, I knew some things from having my hair done over the years, but the retail end of running a hair salon was uncharted territory to both of us. By the time we realized how steep the learning curve was, we were already in too deep to back out; so, like we always do in our life and marriage, we took the bull by the horns. Manuela decided she would need to become a hairstylist, so she studied to earn her hairdressers license while simultaneously running the business. In a relatively short period of time, she began to build up a decent clientele.

Early on in this venture, it became apparent that the franchise was not going to help us to achieve any sizable sales. Their marketing strategy was about offering incentive coupons, so we were essentially providing our services for free, in hopes that it would create a clientele of repeat customers. We diligently tracked our sales, and while our business did grow, our overhead was very costly. We had opened just before Christmas, which should have been our busiest season, but while our sales were good, we did not make the returns we expected. We quickly learned that the franchise was full of unfulfilled promises, starting with our opening day celebration, which they did not even bother to show up for.

Mike didn't waste time getting out of the franchise as soon as we'd made enough rounds to terminate the relationship. As it turned out, most of the other franchisees followed suit within a few months. We changed the name of our business and the marketing strategies we used. It wasn't long before we began to see positive results.

The location of our salon presented an additional obstacle, since it was in an area that was already saturated with hair salons. Clients would come for a freebie, but they rarely returned. We knew we would have to work hard to make this business take off on its wings.

We ran the salon for eight years, adding other services over time, such as esthetics and tanning. Mike came in on evenings and weekends to do the books, and Manuela was cutting hair and taking overflow when stylist turnover was high. We even redesigned the entire space to make it look less like the discount *chop shop* it had been when we first took over. At a time when many businesses were ramping down because of the introduction of a new sales tax, Mike decided to do the opposite, and we completely renovated the salon, changed our marketing, and ramped up our business. It was the best year we ever had. Things slowly started to improve.

The business was open seven days a week for the first six years. We tried to take Sundays off, but our staff tended to call in sick, or they would say it was too busy to handle alone, and we'd end up back in the shop. After a while, we decided to just close on Sundays, and that was one of the best decisions we ever made. It didn't affect our bottom line noticeably, and the reduction in expenses compensated for any lost profits. Best of all, we finally had a day to ourselves again!

Things got even better when we eventually brought in a *chair renter*. This stylist brought his own clientele, purchased his own products, and provided us with steady monthly revenue in the form of a rental fee for the space.

Eight years into this venture, things were going really well, but then lady luck sent us a message that it was time for a change in the form of an offer we couldn't refuse. The messenger was a person who kept walking into the salon and saying, *"I heard you are for sale."* We always replied that we weren't actually looking to sell, but after the fourth or fifth time this happened we finally told them to make us an offer. We were happy with the business, but we figured that selling might not be such a bad idea after all, if the price is right, and we guessed it would be, given the level of interest this person was expressing.

The buyer made us an offer, and feeling a mixture of relief and sadness at the thought of letting go of this business that had defined our lives for eight years, we handed them the keys and wished them luck. It was difficult to let go at first, as we had some really awesome staff and fantastic clients, many of whom we still keep in touch with to this day. However, the reality was that we needed a change, and with the wealth of experience we had gained, we knew we were ready to take on much more.

It had been a difficult and tiring eight years, but I will never regret my experience with the salon because the learning I gained from it was invaluable. I now understand the service and retail industry, and I have a new skill—cutting and styling hair—that I will keep forever. I also learned to lead by example. Only experience can offer you such an education in life.

The Right Staff

In business, it's vital to find the right people to work with and for you. Finding the right associates and employees can be an art in itself, and it is one well worth perfecting, because you need people who are willing and able to provide the support and loyalty you need and command.

Get to know your staff, appreciate them, and give them a sense of partnership with you, but also remember that business is business. Mike always asks that employees earn his trust through their actions, results, and customer satisfaction. Some people can talk a good game, but they fail in the delivery. When people do earn your trust, however, it is important to recognize and reward them for their efforts in a way that you know is meaningful for *them*. In a very real sense, good employees are your business partners, and you need to treat them as such.

Mike has a great *what makes them tick* radar that helps him enhance his relationship with his employees. This means that he takes the time to learn the strengths and weaknesses of each worker so he can be sure to place them where they fit best, and reward them in a way that reflects who they are.

Over the years, we have built some amazing teams of employees and partners to help develop our business ventures. Mike especially likes to dwell on individual strengths to offset weakness, to build our power teams. It is like the divide and conquer approach to team building, whereby each player brings something unique to the table that compliments other team members. One member's weakness is another member's strength, and can be a very powerful combination.

A great example of this can be found in two people who worked for our computer company in the past. The first—we'll call him Jack—could repair a computer like nobody's business, but his interpersonal skills were somewhat on the shy side. On more than one occasion, customers called asking when he was going to show up, because Jack had gone in, fixed the problem, and left without saying hardly a word to anyone! The second technician—we'll call him Bill—could talk his way out of a lion's den, with a new fur coat to boot, but he wasn't always able to fix the problem. However, despite the fact that he was not necessarily the best technician, Bill got better customer reviews than Jack, who actually fixed the problem. Mike has learned that it pays to take note of these individual strengths and weaknesses that every employee brings to the company. It allows him to give them what they need in order to do their jobs better and compliment other team members. Take the time to understand your people, and they will work much harder for you.

Mike knew that Jack had difficulty socializing. In fact, Jack never came to company Christmas parties because he was too anxious about going up on stage to receive his service reward. Mike knew it was useless to reward someone in a way they don't want; he knew that putting Jack on stage to receive a service pin was like smacking him across the chops with a dead fish. However, giving him a pat on the back in private, or a discrete mention in a staff meeting, brought a smile to his face every time. Get to know your staff, and treat them according to their needs, and you will get far better results. If an employee does something special, I have no problem sending them and their partner for a nice dinner, picking up some show tickets, or some other small gift that they will appreciate, to show my gratitude. By getting their input on decisions that impact them, you create a sense of ownership that inspires them to contribute. No matter how small or large an employee's contribution, appropriate recognition from you will strengthen your relationship with them to everyone's benefit.

Make Things Happen by Listening to Your Gut

When opportunity knocks, at least answer the door! You never know where it may lead. Sometimes the best business opportunities arrive out of the blue, so be prepared to make a quick decision when chance comes calling.

Mike learned at an early stage to listen to his gut when it came to investing. *"Every time I listened to someone else, I lost money,"* he says. *"A deal is not a deal until the money is in the bank."* We have seen many deals in which someone has said "Yes, yes, yes," but then the whole thing fell through in the end. There are a lot of people out there selling bones with no meat on them to packs of investors starving for profits. No matter how bright and shiny the deal seems to be in its beginning, the ultimate proof is money in the bank. We approach all our business dealings with this in mind, and we are cautious about over-extending our finances until we know that the deal will close for sure. Of course, we spend a lot of time on due diligence, but that time is well spent because that is how you limit loss and improve profits.

When Mike first moved to Vancouver, in 1978, he was young, single, and travelled a great deal for work. He was renting a basement apartment, but he hated paying rent because, in his eyes, it's money down the toilet to line someone else's pocket—especially since he was rarely home!

Eventually, Mike started scoping out residential real estate prices in Vancouver. He found that houses there were much more expensive than they were in Ontario, where he was from. So, he decided that if houses were out of range, perhaps he could buy an apartment. He soon discovered that with just a ten percent down payment, his mortgage would be equivalent to what he was paying in rent, and he'd eventually own his own place. Excited at the prospect of becoming a homeowner, he told his friends and family of his plans, and guess what? Every last one of them tried to talk him out of it, because they simply couldn't see how buying an apartment could be a wise move. They told him he was crazy to consider it, and he listened.

Of course, he now realizes he shouldn't have—that apartment nearly doubled in price in two years. Mike lost out on a valuable investment but gained an even more valuable lesson: always listen to yourself, not the naysayers around you. By the time he had a chance to get into real estate again, he had to move further out from Vancouver to Burnaby, in order to find properties he could afford.

Like so many people, Mike also learned the hard way when it came to investing in the stock market. He took a correspondence securities course, then set up a trading account with a local brokerage firm. Since he was new to investing, he put in only what he could afford to lose: $1,000. He figured that it'd be great if he made money, but if he lost, he'd consider it a thousand dollar lesson and move on. His very first investment was in British Petroleum, on the advice of his broker. It was a new listing at the time, and very promising. In three days, he sold the stock he'd bought in BP for a 25% profit. Encouraging to say the least!

Emboldened by this initial success, Mike started researching and purchasing stocks on his own. At first, he bought a variety of stocks, with hit and miss results. He quickly learned that hot stock tips from brokers and friends either never panned out or were highly volatile at best. He'd have to watch those stocks like a hawk in order to make money from them. Whether because of this or in spite of it, Mike soon got to the point where he was comfortable following market trends and making his trading decisions based on them.

Eventually, Mike managed to find a stock that had a steady rollercoaster trend, and he followed it for quite some time. Based on this long-term trend, he decided to borrow $5,000 to invest in this stock at a moment when timing was crucial (for the record, he never borrowed to fund a stock purchase again). Because he understood the market so well, he bought this stock at the low end and sold when it was near its peak, making enough money to pay off his first mortgage. The stock continued to skyrocket, and yes, he could have made a lot more money, but he was happy because he'd achieved his goal of becoming mortgage-free.

In the 1980s, stock trading was very different from how it is today. Today's investors have the benefit of technology and the internet, but back then, Mike was tracking trends with The Globe and Mail, then plugging what he got from their reports into a Lotus 123 computer program. *"I was mostly trading options, which meant that I was calling my broker several times a day for quotes,"* he says. It was time-consuming to say the least, and eventually, his enthusiasm for trading subsided as a result. By then, however, his efforts had already paid off handsomely, and he was ready to move on to bigger things, with a solid financial base behind him.

Give Up Your Day Job?

Okay, maybe don't quit your day job just yet. However, do make every effort to ensure that you spend your days doing what you love to do. You may need to keep working that day job until you gain the skills and/or training to strike out in a new direction, but just make sure you're taking those steps. Manuela and I are never afraid to get our hands dirty and learn what we need to know to do the job at hand, and we have always found that each new venture leads us to a new and better career.

My own career has taken a very non-linear path. I studied both electronics and business in college, then moved to Vancouver, where I got a job as an IT service technician. I worked for just over twelve years with this company, eventually becoming the service manager for Western Canada. I started my first micro-business on the side, doing woodworking and cabinetry for friends and relatives. I didn't make a lot of money at it, but I learned a ton, and it paid for my tools. After twelve years with the same company, I received an unsolicited job offer to work for another company as their IT manager. I struggled to decide how to proceed, because by now, I really wanted to get into my own business full time. Since I didn't have a defined business plan yet, however, I committed for one to two years, making it clear that I intended to pursue my own projects after that time.

A little more than a year later, I was visiting one of my previous business associates whom I used to purchase IT training courses from. Over time, we had become good friends and stayed in touch. He had recently left his job to open a private business college with another partner. At the time of this meeting, he was having difficulty opening a new location in New Westminster, BC, but he had already opened up locations in Vancouver, Victoria, and Chilliwack. It struck me that this could be a great opportunity to help him out, while at the same time learning the business, so I offered to help him get this new location up and running. I wore many hats, working in admissions, teaching, administration, and management, to learn as much about the business as I could. We had agreed that if I liked the work, I would become a partner and help my friend run this school. I figured there wasn't much of a downside, and I had a lot to gain if all went well. As it turned out, this was one of the best business decisions I had ever made.

So, after opening the Surrey school, I ran it for nine years. Of all the schools my friend started, it was the only location to make a profit within its first year of operation. But it wasn't just beginner's luck; over time, I grew the school to be the second largest in sales, contributing nearly half of the total profits of all locations combined, of which there were now ten.

One night, about seven years later, I was working late with my two partners, putting together a proposal for a government-sponsored training program. After a long day's work and a dinner break, one of my partners commented to my other partner, *"If we only had x thousands of dollars, we could buy out the franchise partner."* I thought about this for a moment, and replied, *"Would x thousand dollars less a bit do the job?"* As it turned out, it did, and I soon became the owner of a one-third interest in the Victoria school, with an option for another school if I wanted it. I had not planned to become involved in another school, but the opportunity was there, so I figured, why not? I originally viewed it as a loan to help the school out, but two years later, I sold it back and doubled my money, plus they paid me interest on the original loan. Not a bad deal at all, especially since I had borrowed from my line of credit using the bank's money, so it really did not cost me anything at all!

Despite my successes with the school, however, I kept getting drawn back into IT. At this time, there was no consistency between how schools were run at each location, and because of this, things were always breaking down. With my background in computers, I did most of my own IT work myself, which kept things relatively stable. I also helped out the other schools whenever I could. Then, one day, during one of our many planning sessions, the subject of IT support came up again, and one of my partners suggested that since I had an IT background, perhaps I would consider a change in role. By this time, I was ready, and welcomed this change with open arms.

So it was that I founded my IT support company, and my primary objective was to provide support to all of the schools. However, I also had enough flexibility to seek other clients, and in this way, my company did grow over time. While we mostly specialized in schools and large-scale deployments, we also took on new customers in professional services, such as accounting firms and law firms. From the other chapters though, you know that eventually, after looking after everyone else's problems for so many years, I needed to make a change and look after myself. Something was going to break, and I didn't want it to be me. This is when I found, quite by chance, the investment course that has led us to where we are today.

For me, being self-employed has always been an interesting challenge that I thoroughly enjoyed. Every day is different; I have never had a set schedule, and at this point, I don't think I could adapt to one. The freedom I enjoy, and the flexibility I have to do my own thing, have been worth all the blood, sweat, and tears I have poured into this lifestyle, and I wouldn't have it any other way. I once told someone that I will not be caged, and that if anyone ever tries to put me in a cage, I will break out. I need to be in charge of my own destiny like I need to eat, drink, and breathe, and so should you. If you must work for someone else, just be sure you're doing something you love, and that you are well-compensated for it. No matter how happy you might be with your current situation, however, I say to always keep an eye out for the opportunities that lurk around every corner, especially where you least expect them. You never know when you'll be given the chance to take a more direct route to your dreams.

For her part, Manuela also finds being self-employed exhilarating. She describes her experience of it this way: *"Nothing compares to the rush I felt when we closed our first deal as property investors—no drug could re-create that sensation. Preparing the house for the new tenants, handing them the keys, and visiting them a week later with a house warming gift gave me such a feeling of satisfaction in our ability to create happiness for this new family. I couldn't wait to do the next one, and another one after that, and on and on…making a lot of people happy in the process."*

Don't Let Opportunity Pass You By

Mike and I recently heard a story, which we felt had merit in sharing it with you. It's about how one business entrepreneur, when they were first getting started, succeeded with a product, while another business entrepreneur and the same exact product fell on their back sides! They were at a trade show representing their products, and when the doors opened to the public, one was standing and positioned at their table's edge as the other was seated at their table. As flocks of retailers were passing by, the entrepreneur standing decided they needed to catch those passing by, and yelled out, *"Let me show you how my product will change your bottom line!"* The business owner, seated at his table, remained seated, never speaking out or acknowledging anyone as they walked past his table, remaining content to just wait for someone to hand him an order. At the end of the day, those that had gone after the opportunity in front of them, were the winners. The business owner who remained seated, ignoring opportunity, ended his day with his budget in the red, and the other went to the bank!

I have attended many trade shows as an exhibitor, and it amazes me how many exhibitors spend a small fortune to attend the event, and yet do not follow up afterwards. During the event, we always made an effort to meet as many people as we could, and to collect their business cards for a draw.

Where possible, I would write notes on their cards, so I could do a more personalized follow- up afterwards. Prior to the trade show, I usually made a series of follow-up emails so that all I needed to do was collect their email addresses and send it off the following day. This is another opportunity to contact them, re-introduce our products and services, announce the prize draw winner, and offer any show specials. If you do this right, you will increase your new business opportunities dramatically.

Bottom Line

Mike and I know that any successful business takes time, effort, commitment, and patience. Don't let it stagnate; continually evaluate and adjust to keep it working. In fact, it doesn't hurt to put that principle to work for everything in your life! Never be afraid to mix things up in new ways in your efforts to get things working again, no matter what form your business takes. There is no such thing as failure, unless you believe there is—we all make mistakes, but learning from them, and then fixing them, takes a bit more effort. In our lives as investors and entrepreneurs, we've found that there is far more satisfaction in learning and fixing than in just walking away. Any lazy bum can walk away from a business *failure*, but the great ones know how to be humbled without being broken. Like Peter Pan said, you can fly if you believe you can, no matter how unlikely it may seem! The secret is to never stop learning, be grateful for the lessons, and apply what you learn as if your life depends on it, because it does. That's our philosophy in a nutshell!

Chapter 4
The Kiss That Changed Our World

**WE THOUGHT IT WAS ODD, BUT WE DO NOT USE TRANSIT VERY OFTEN, SO WE FIGURED WE SHOULD FOLLOW THE RULES......
QUESTION THOUGH: WHO DO YOU KISS IF YOU TRAVEL ALONE?**

Chapter 4
The Kiss That Changed Our World

"It is not in the stars to hold our destiny, but in ourselves."
– William Shakespeare

You just never know when a moment will come that changes the course of your life forever. It happened for us when, on a trip from Istanbul to Dubai, we decided to take a one-day excursion to the ancient ruins of Petra, where Manuela was met with affection.

Settled by desert traders, known as the Nabateans, in the fourth century B.C., Petra is located between the Red and the Dead Seas, and was lost to Western civilization for 500 years. When we realized we would be passing so close to it, Manuela and I simply knew we had to see it. Half-built and half-carved into rose-colored sandstone, it is a UNESCO World Heritage site, and a sculptural masterpiece. Petra is truly one of the world's most breathtaking archaeological sites, and it is also where Manuela kissed ZuZu, and changed our lives forever.

What's in a Name?

First, I should let you know that ZuZu is a camel, and kissing a camel is not something many people can boast of doing, if any can at all! But I've always known Manuela wasn't like anyone else...ZuZu was lying down, which put him at eye-level with Manuela, and her flashy fingernails caught his attention. He laid his soft fat lips on her nails, in the camel equivalent of a gallant knight kissing the fingers of his fair lady. Camels are not known for their even temperament, but in response, Manuela reached out and began petting ZuZu's cheeks. Then, moved by some ancient, unknowable force, she bent down and kissed that camel on the nose!

 Camels are known as *nature's true nomads*, so perhaps ZuZu recognized a kindred spirit when he saw the wanderlust in Manuela's heart. Or perhaps, as animals often do, he just picked up on her caring and loving nature. Kissing that huge animal on the nose was a big risk, but ZuZu responded by sweetly lifting his face toward Manuela like an adoring puppy, and in that moment, he became our property company's new mascot and namesake. Just as ZuZu the camel was proof that not all camels are ornery, at ZuZu Properties, we prove that the process of owning, selling, or investing in real estate can be easy, comfortable, and beneficial for everyone involved. We find joy in helping people realize their life goals and dreams, in the most stress-free way possible.

Our Mission

When a client comes to us with a dream of financial security or home ownership, it is one of our greatest joys to help them find ways to make those dreams a reality. There is always more than one path to success and happiness, and it's our mission to help those who are prepared to work in order to follow their dreams, and our privilege to find the best fit for them. Our lifelong interest in real estate and property investment started when I was just out of college, and I let my friends and family talk me out of buying a one-bedroom apartment in Vancouver. It was the biggest mistake of my life! Within two years, that apartment had almost doubled in value. It was a hard lesson, but I've never forgotten it.

Since then, Manuela and I have been successful investors in real estate, as well as in other areas. We've started and run thriving businesses, and we've owned several homes together. I bought my first house in 1983; then we bought our first home together in 1987, and purchased our current home in 2002. In 2011, we began investing in revenue properties, learning from and working with programs similar to those we now offer. Then, with the help of a certain camel, we established ZuZu Properties, in 2014.

You see, we believe that home ownership is a dream everyone should be able to realize, with a bit of willpower, foresight, and intestinal fortitude. A person's home should be their sanctuary from the craziness of everyday life. Owning the roof over your head, and putting your money into a space that's truly yours, provides emotional security, as well as financial rewards. At the very least, it helps build a nest egg for retirement, which so many people can ill afford in today's *buy now, pay later* society.

We know that real estate is a sound investment that can offer solid returns over time. It has helped us and our clients enjoy a lifestyle that allows us to travel to fascinating places, where we meet interesting people and wonderful creatures, including ZuZu the camel. If we can help even a few people realize their dreams of home ownership, we will know we have done something worthwhile with our lives. We recognize that traditional mortgage qualifications are designed primarily to serve the needs of the banks, and they too often exclude people, who have the financial capacity to own a home, from reaching that dream.

We're truly grateful to have found a way to help others succeed. Best of all, the financial security of being a property owner can provide people with the nudge they need to get out and explore the world and expand their dreams for their lives. At ZuZu Properties, it is always our goal to provide a service that benefits everyone involved. And as Manuela says, *"The satisfaction that comes from helping others is priceless."*

Re-inventing Our Freedom

Life has dealt us many different hands along the way; they weren't always winning ones, but they taught us that even a losing one can be a positive experience. It's all about perception and how you choose to look at it. The hurt that the experience gave us didn't change, but what we learned from it helped us move forward and turn it into something positive. It didn't necessarily relate to what had happened, but we decided to get back up as quickly as possible, not dwelling on it but moving on.

Mike has always been interested in real estate; not as an agent but as an investor. Unfortunately, he never had an opportunity, until the last few years, to research it more. He retired his computer business and needed something to *occupy* him and make the transition from working crazy long hours less drastic.

He went to a 2-hour real estate investment seminar, came home all excited, and told me that he just signed up for a 3-day course in real estate investment, and that if I wanted to, I could join him, as the offer was for 2 people. I immediately said *yes,* and so our new adventure began.

We took several courses on real estate investment over the course of about a year, and applied our new knowledge immediately. After the first 3-day course, we came back home, and the very next day, we had our first deal. We couldn't believe what was happening, but we were both scared and excited at the same time, not sure if we were doing it right, but we received so much support and mentoring from the course organizers that we decided to just jump in. That first deal opened up our eyes, and that's when we found out how we can help people.

That's when ZuZu Properties was born. We started working on a business model and a website, and we were off. The name ZuZu came from a camel that we met in Petra, Jordan, while visiting that amazing location. He was lying down in the shade, and I approached him with great caution, as I was aware of their temperament and ability to spit at you with great accuracy! ZuZu, however, gave me a great sense of calmness and trust. I looked at his big brown eyes while petting him on the cheeks, and decided to kiss his soft nose. To my amazement, he lifted his head and allowed me to kiss him without any fear. His keeper was in total shock and discouraged me to even touch him at first. But I took a big leap of faith and did it anyway, knowing full well the consequences. This is why we named our business ZuZu Properties. It's about taking risks and getting it done.

The real estate market, in many big cities, is very expensive, and so many new young families can't afford to own their own home to raise their children. Some people have credit issues that they need to repair or rebuild, and some self-employed people can't get a mortgage, as they are required to have a bigger percentage for the down payment. New immigrants also have to wait a few years to get established, or someone just needs to build a minimum down payment. Oftentimes, the income is there, but some people don't know how to manage money or finances. This is something that we see all the time. Some people think that paying cash for everything and not having credit cards is the best thing, but unfortunately, they don't understand that not having a credit history can be detrimental in applying for a mortgage. Lenders want to see that credit report. It's a footprint of how people handle their finances. Some suffered hardships along the way and had to declare bankruptcy, but that doesn't mean they are bad or irresponsible; they just suffered a setback, and are able to show that they are now on the road back to recovery.

So How Do We Help Others?

First, we had to build a team of professionals, such as real estate agents, mortgage brokers, insurance brokers, inspectors, contractors, etc.

We then go through a pre-screening process with the applicants, explaining to them in detail what the program is all about. It's sometimes a harsh reality for them to realize that home ownership isn't a possibility unless their income improves substantially, or they get some credit built up, and clear some debts. If the income is there but they need a bit more time to fix everything else, such as correcting some credit issue or saving for a down payment, we can hopefully help them.

From that point, if they are interested, and we see that the program could be a good fit for them, we give them a shopping list of things they need to do in order to move forward. Once provided, the paperwork goes to a professional mortgage broker for an initial assessment. That said, a mortgage broker will have a direct discussion with them and provide them with a written report designed just for them, on all the steps they need to take to be able to qualify for a mortgage in 1 to 3 years.

Mike, must you always be doing business? Appraisals here too?
Yes, Manuela, what do you think?
Okay then, this is a great investment; the locals will love it.

What we also request from the applicant is a monthly detailed budget. For us, that is a very important piece of information, not only for the numbers on it, but more so to see if they even know what's coming in and going out every month. Also, the way the budget is put together is important. We've seen everything from scribbled numbers on a piece of napkin, to a *"Budget Template Form"* downloaded on the internet. We take a close look at the number to see if they are realistic and make sense. *Napkin budgets* have a lot of information missing, and consist of 4 to 5 list items. That shows us that often people don't have a clue where their money is going. The real budget itemizes every single dollar coming in and going out. For us, it's a reflection of the person preparing it. We want to see that they know exactly what their financial situation is.

Once that is done, and the mortgage broker has had a chance to review the documents and has talked to the applicants about qualifying for a mortgage down the road, we will then let the realtor know to take the applicant *shopping*. There will be, however, a spending budget on the property. They can only look at real estate within a certain price range, not exceeding the number that the mortgage broker gave them while qualifying them for a mortgage. There also has to be room for property appreciation over a couple of years, so a fair margin has to be considered upon the initial purchase.

Once they find an appropriate property at a suitable price, in their acceptable geographical area, we then step in and negotiate the purchase. A qualified inspector will go and do a full property inspection and submit a detailed report on the findings. If the property shows a lot of big issues, such as roof, mold, signs of leaks inside the walls and flooring, we will go back to the seller and address those issues and adjust the price accordingly, to the value of the repairs. If there are issues with foundations, we will walk away from the property.

We want our clients to move into a safe home with, hopefully, not too many surprises along the way. They will live there as temporary tenants but hopefully will be able to call it their home in a span of a couple of years. We don't like to call them tenants, as they really are *"owners in training."* For the duration of the tenancy, they will pay a rent amount that will have to cover the mortgage and other costs associated with the property. They will also pay an additional amount every month, which will be put towards their down payment at the end of the contract. Once the contract reaches the dates agreed upon, and they have followed all the steps required by the mortgage broker to be successful in qualifying, we will sign over the title of the property to them, and they will be home owners. They are essentially buying back the house from ZuZu Properties, at a specific time, for a pre-agreed upon price, which should not be higher than their mortgage qualifications initially established by the mortgage broker. What we hope for is that the property will be valued at more than the final purchase price, in which case the *tenants/owners* will already have some equity built in with the buy-back.

There is a great amount of satisfaction when the day finally comes; the program has gone full circle, and the process has been successful for everyone involved. There are always some hiccups along the way, but we always manage to find ways of dealing with the challenges that life throws in the way. We are determined to have our clients succeed and become home owners. Mike and I follow their progress regularly to make sure they are on track and have followed the required steps. This is why our initial screening process is so important. We don't want to give anyone false hopes, take their money, and wait for them to fail at the end.

Rent-to-own is only a portion of what we do in the real estate world. We aren't afraid to look behind new doors to see what opportunity we could find. We have rental properties as well, with excellent tenants. We are also now looking at some commercial properties and land development opportunities. Every day, we come across new and different opportunities, which we always investigate, as one never knows where they will lead!

We wished we had discovered this real estate investment world many years ago. We truly enjoy it, and the best part is that we can do it from anywhere in the world. We don't need a *business* location, as we work from home, and all we need is a telephone and internet access. We have signed documents, contracts, offers, and much more, via internet from all corners of the world, and nobody even knew it. This is the beauty of this type of business; you can conduct it from anywhere!

Mike and Manuela, who dared to dream in the beginning, say never to give up on yourselves or limit that which you can reach, remembering to step outside your comfort zone for a larger slice of this wonderful life that's possible…If you keep on dreaming and pushing your stretch for a better life, anything is possible.

Mike, do you really believe we can rent-to-own this building too?
Sure, Manuela; you know we have always said anything is possible.

Chapter 5
Living by Example

AHHH..I'M NOT SURE THIS IS A GOOD IDEA!
OKAY, I'LL HANG ON AND SMILE FOR THE CAMERA
BUT ZUZU DOESN'T LOOK HAPPY

Chapter 5
Living by Example

Mike and I believe that what you put into life will dictate or set the outcome of your own destiny. We have had a fortunate life, finding love and respect for one another, and though times were difficult at the beginning, with commitment and hard work, we have prevailed and have overcome the financial struggles we once had. Because of our good fortune, and knowledge of how to gain control of your financial world, we have made the decision to help as many people as possible, as long as they are willing to work hard and stay focused on their dream, and be ready to do whatever they need to in order to succeed.

The Jennifer and Dale Story

We have also chosen a few stories of individuals that made such a sacrifice, and conquered their own milestones.

Our first story is about Jennifer and Dale. If you, too, feel compelled to reach out to us, we are ready to assist you as well. Congratulations Jennifer and Dale!

Mike and I have dedicated our efforts to helping anyone who wants to own their own home, by creating our Rent-to-Own Guidelines. It gives us that fuzzy warm feeling that makes us glow from within when we find a couple that wants to work for their home but sadly gets rejected by traditional mortgage requirements. Many come to us with no hope, yet try hard not to despair or give up. Rejection is difficult under any circumstances, but if those that come to us are willing to do the homework, we give them a way to get into the game; we will go to the mat to help them.

We have many success stories like Jennifer and Dale's, and we want to share these stories with you, so that you, too, can see—by having the attitude to *never give up*—you, too, can be a winner!

When Jennifer and Dale first met with us, they were one of our earlier rent-to-own clients. Mike and I developed a large investor network of real estate professionals, and one of our real estate agents referred them to us after having tried to help them buy a townhome, which they had felt they could afford but were not able to get the financing they needed.

Jennifer and Dale were very hard workers in life, but even with Dale working at a meat packing company, and Jennifer working in a warehouse for pet food and supplies, their life was anything but easy. Saving for a down payment was difficult due to not having a solid plan for a budget, but once they had guidance, they soared. They had come from a tough background of hard times, relationships, and marriages, yet determination gave them a spark in their eyes, which both Mike and I recognized, and we yearned to help them.

We also wanted to be sure they were willing to go the distance and not fizzle out at the first sign of hard work so we gave them—what may appear to be impossible assignments, and expected them to take a while to complete. To our surprise, they not only completed what we asked of them but in amazing time! They were tired of paying rent and not having any rights and/or say in their living circumstances. Jennifer wanted something with a garden, and to be able to enjoy the great outdoors, where they could play with their two small dogs!

But they had real problems when we first met. They only knew the life of living from paycheck to paycheck, had no down payment, and had bad credit. But that was not the worst of their bad luck. They owed back taxes and lived literally from day to day.

Although Mike and I had seen this kind of trouble with others, we had a feeling about this couple, and followed our instincts to help them. We then discovered that Dale was a loving and trusting family man who had been working to support his family by giving them cheques, at times far exceeding what was required, not realizing that his share to support them was only 50% of the costs for braces, clothes, sports activities, and living expenses, apart from the general child care maintenance, or other needs for his children. They were ultimately taking advantage of his kind loving spirit to do what was right in life, with him never asking to see receipts they claimed as expenses, but instead, paying what was asked for, without question. Both Jennifer and Dale were employed and working at demanding jobs, but they were still unable to make ends meet, and this situation certainly did not help!

Although they did have steady employment, on paper, they were a risk that no lender would take, and they ached to be home owners, willing to do anything, and prepared to do whatever it took to accomplish their dreams!

Realizing their dreams of home ownership was very clear, but how hard were they willing to work? Although Jennifer appeared to us as a bit rough around the edges, we soon discovered it was only because she had not yet become comfortable with us. That was understandable, as we were strangers to them; and we were asking them questions to learn private information so we could ascertain what our position would be in helping them secure their dream home. It was not long after that we became interested in taking a chance, and Jennifer relaxed, opening up to us with their story.

We were not quite sure why we had felt this strong interest to take on their plight for help, as we knew that no one else would consider either one of them as rent-to-own material, or any other form of home ownership.

However, we were not in the business of just handing over any property without a lot of work and proof of sincerity from our clients. We gave them what we called homework, which would show us if they were willing to buckle down and work for their dream. Most of our clients we meet fail to complete this important step, not realizing this is actually part of the qualification process.

The way we look at it is if they are not willing to put the effort into doing their homework, or spending $25 to get their credit report, they are probably not motivated enough to stick with the program. So, off they went to round up their credit score reports, their last two years' tax reports, copies of their pay stubs, and letters from their employers. They were also asked to prepare a budget and they did this in record time.

While they were doing their homework, Mike and I continued to search for their home that fit the criteria for them. The first townhouse we had found for them was snapped up by someone else, so we lost that opportunity, but we continued to look for something suitable and within their budget. Three houses later, we found another townhouse.

We were still concerned about another hurdle they needed to resolve, and it was for a down payment. Jennifer and Dale had no savings, and it was bothersome as to what we could do without it, but not only had they completed their assignments, they had managed to tighten their belts and save something for a down payment, though not quite enough.

This demonstrated to us how motivated and committed to succeed they were. The townhouse we found needed repairs and minor renovations, but rather than pay someone to do the work for us, they both jumped in and said that they would do as much of the renovations themselves as they could.

We gave them a budget to work from, and they ran around town to find the best deals possible, with great success.

They literally shopped until they dropped, finding appliances, vanities, paint, carpeting, and many other bits and pieces needed for their future home.

In fact, they came in under their budget, and we had enough left over to throw in new flooring for the kitchen and hallway.

They put in, as we call it, sweat equity, towards their initial down payment, and they worked like beavers getting everything done. We even rolled up our own sleeves to dig in! They worked night and day to complete the renovations in time, plus they also had to pack up their belongings to move into their new dream home. Moving day came, and they were so happy with their decision; finally, they had something they could both call home, and it was all theirs.

During the course of their rent-to-own program, which was typically a 3-year term, we monitored their progress, making adjustments as necessary to build their credit and save for their down payment.

How many landlords do you know that would show up at their tenant's door with a bottle of wine in one hand and a case of beer in the other? They were fantastic tenants, always paying their rent on time, and a joy to work with.

They also continued to improve their home, upgrading the washer and dryer, renovating their upstairs bathroom, and so on.

Jennifer got her dream of having a small garden and taking advantage of the outdoors, and they set up a seating area in front of their unit, surrounded by flowers.

They got involved in their new community, taking the time to talk and get to know their neighbors. They became like the watch dogs of the complex, monitoring suspicious activities, and reporting crimes and unlawful events to the strata company and the council members. They took the time to meet and talk to all the residents, and it made a big impact on crime and illegal activities in the complex.

Bad tenants were reported and dealt with accordingly. Slowly, that small community was looking better by the day.

Dale took on an extra part time job, doing landscaping on weekends, and working overtime when possible at his regular job. After three years, they managed to continue to save for their down payment and build their credit.

They now qualified for a mortgage, and completed the purchase of their home. To celebrate, we took Jennifer and Dale out for dinner at a local German restaurant. You have never seen two happier people, and for us…we are so proud of their accomplishment—it's moments like this that bring us so much pride in what we do.

Being able to help people, like Jennifer and Dale, makes it all worthwhile, and we would definitely do it again.

Jennifer and Dale are getting married next April, and they invited us both to share in their special day. We know they will be successful in their new home, and we made some wonderful new friends in the process.

Jennifer has a wonderful sense of humor, and her favorite way to communicate is through text messaging. She had us in stitches every time she would contact us for something.

When it was official for them to take possession, we made sure to let them know that life throws us a curve ball sometimes, and if this was the case for them, and they were having some difficulty, to let us know. There is no way we would want them to lose their home after all the effort they put into to getting it. No matter what happens, we would be there to help them.

And the Story Continues

In addition to Jennifer and Dale, we have helped a young woman in her twenties, who was a new immigrant from Asia. After moving to Canada, she was helping her mom financially; unfortunately, she came across hard times and had to declare bankruptcy. She worked at a big box store, but because her wages were paid based on commission, she needed a larger down payment to qualify for a mortgage. She was renting a condominium and really liked where she was living. The commuter train was within a 5-minute walk from her home, and because she did not own a car, that feature was important to her, making the desire to own the condominium where she was living, even more desirable.

She, too, demonstrated just how motivated and committed she was to own her own home. She had already shown how good she was at saving money, but because she was still a new citizen to Canada, working a commission based job and having bruised credit, she needed more time to qualify for a mortgage. Luckily, a unit became available for purchase in her building shortly after we met her, and we moved ahead with an offer to purchase it. We had a good feeling about this young woman, so listening to our instincts again, we went ahead with the purchase. Our offer was accepted, and everything was in place shortly afterwards. We had signed a 3-year term with her as well, but shortly after she moved in her new condominium, she had sadly been laid off work, as the company was going out of business.

We were worried for her, but she wasn't at all! She assured us that she had other savings that would keep her for at least 6–8 months without any problem. Well, being the little beaver that she is, she found new employment almost immediately, in a high-end department store, in downtown Vancouver. Her remuneration package was sweeter than her previous employment, and she was also earning bonuses. This young woman loved her new job, and after 2 years in the rent-to-own program, she asked if she could complete the agreement early. She earned a better income than before, and was able to save a considerable amount of money since beginning her new job.

After she repaired her credit, she was now able to qualify a whole year ahead of schedule. We amended the paperwork, and off she went on her merry way, a very happy and grateful young woman, with the experience of the program and a relationship we had garnered together.

We still communicate on social media, and we see that she has traveled a fair amount since working in the department store. She always exceeds her goals and is rewarded with trips everywhere in the world, all expenses paid. Another happy ending for all concerned!

Those are just a couple of the success stories that we have. We have helped many other couples and single people, all with their own stories, but the common link was in always not having enough for a down payment, or not much in the way of a savings account, and poor credit.

We are happy to say that they are all on their way to becoming successful home owners.

One couple was supposed to qualify a month ago, and they were doing amazingly well. They both had started new jobs when we first met them, and during the 3 years that followed, their jobs got better, with both of them getting raises every time we talked. They always made their payments on time, and we never had any issues or concerns with them. So, 2 months prior to them finishing the program, we were in the process of lining everything up for a smooth takeover when we noticed that both of their credit scores took a nose dive, just 3 months before completion. We gasped at the findings and asked them to explain what had happened. They had decided to go and purchase a new vehicle, authorizing the dealerships that they visited to pull their credit. They didn't realize of the gravity of their actions.

When the mortgage broker was shopping for a lender to take their mortgage, they would turn them down, as their debt ratio was too high, and they were considered as a high risk. We were so surprised at what they had done. They were doing so well building their credit and paying down their existing debt. They obviously didn't think of the consequences and got caught up in the moment. This little setback could have cost them their home and everything they put towards the down payment in the lease option agreement. We know that some companies out there would have pulled the rug out from under their feet and put them out to pasture for breaching the contract. We didn't want to do that. We sat down with them and came up with a solution. We were able to extend the 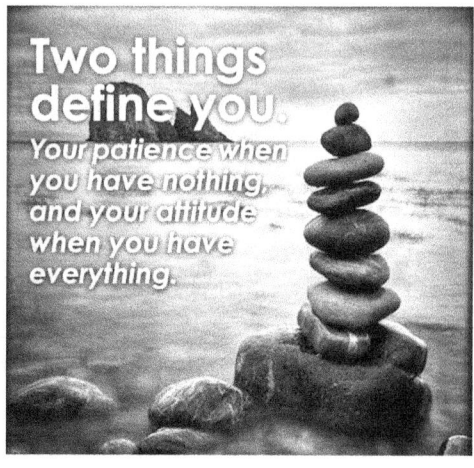 mortgage on their home for another year, and recalculate the payments and expenses accordingly. We had to rewrite some of the contracts to meet new standards and regulations from governing agencies on lease options.

In the next 12 months, they were required to sell the new vehicle they had just bought, trading it in for something much cheaper, or even used, to reduce the debt substantially, bringing the prior debt down considerably, and to rebuild their credit, without having anyone pull it.

They were visibly shocked to learn of the consequences of their actions. They promised to do whatever was necessary to fix it, and were very grateful for a second chance. We aren't heartless and don't want to leave them homeless, but they had to see, hear, and understand that it could have cost them their home—a home that they picked in the construction stage, located in a beautiful and quiet part of town, for their now 5-year-old child to grow up in. We are confident that they will be successful in completing the program next year.

Not All Stories Have a Happy Ending

We got a call once from a mortgage broker who was trying to help a couple who was currently in a lease option that was due to end within the next month, only to be told at the last minute that they weren't going to qualify for a mortgage.

This is where the ugly and greedy side of business shows its true colors. For the prior 3 years, they were living in a home that they thought would be theirs one day. They both had great jobs with substantial incomes, and weren't living above their means at all—no fancy cars, no big screen TVs in every room, no expensive furniture, or priceless art. When we went to see them at their home, it looked like they were living with the bare minimums and low budget.

From what we understood by reviewing the documents, they hadn't gone through a qualifying process, explaining in detail what they would need to do during the period of the lease option in order to be able to take over the mortgage at the end.

They were making their regular payments every month, gave a good down payment at the beginning, and continued to pay towards the option. Those people were set up for failure, as they didn't receive any guidance and/or help during the 3-year period. We tried to help them save their home, but unfortunately, the price to purchase it from the company on title was too much, as it needed a fair amount of work inside and outside, and even inside the walls to repair leaks from the roof.

We were saddened by their situation; they not only lost their dream but also all the extra monies that they paid up front and throughout the 3 years. We can't always help everyone, but we like to at least try, even if it's just for giving ideas on finding a solution to proceed further, or maybe at a later date. Sadly, we were unable to find a way to help them.

We have seen other investors grant loans to those who have no possibility of succeeding. It was obvious to us that they were setting their tenants up for failure, and lining their own pockets. In fact, in some locations, rent-to-own is now illegal because unscrupulous investors have caused so much damage. A good friend of ours once said, *"Don't be greedy; there is more than enough to go around."* The fact of the matter is that people who lean this way are never satisfied, and likely lead unhappy lives. We are firm believers in the old adage, *it is better to give than receive,* and can easily look at ourselves in the mirror and feel good about what we do.

*"Successful people are always looking for opportunities to help others.
Unsuccessful people are always asking, 'What's in it for me?'"*
– Brian Tracy

Rent-To-Own Background

The purpose for us to do rent-to-own or lease option investments (same things, different wording) was to first and foremost help people in achieving their dream of home ownership, sooner than they normally would. We would put them through what we call our *Owners in Training* program. They would choose their own home, as long as it fit their need geographically, and their budget. We have seen and talked to other investors doing lease options, and all they care about is to have their clients fail at the end of the term so they can keep their money and reclaim the property.

Those investors give a bad name and reputation to rent-to-own programs, and to other investors that are actually trying to help their clients by setting them up for success, rather than failure. We are very diligent and forthcoming when we talk to potential clients.

This program is not suitable for all clients, and not all clients will qualify. If we do not think they will qualify, we take the time to explain to them why it can't be done at this time. We also give them suggestions on what they need to do to be able to qualify at a later time, whether it be because of insufficient income, debt ratio vs income, credit, etc. We offer referrals for help and guidance, so they have something to take away and think about how they could improve their situation.

Chapter 6
Life Waits for No One

Look Manuela… No hands!
Yeah, Mike… The Dead Sea—with all of this salt, we will never sink!

Chapter 6
Life Waits for No One

*"We must let go of the life we have planned,
so as to accept the one that is waiting for us."*
– Joseph Campbell

They say that what doesn't break us makes us stronger, and for Mike and I, perhaps that's especially true. Although we've been dealt our fair share of heartbreaks and setbacks, we always find a way to rally and come out ahead. We truly believe that life is what you make it, and that belief has helped us to make our life as interesting and fulfilling as we can dream it to be. In sharing our stories here, we hope to help you realize that we are never given more than we can handle…that indeed, every experience serves to make us who we are destined to become in life. The trick is to keep saying *yes* to life, no matter what happens.

What Makes Us Stronger

Both Mike and I lost our fathers at a young age. My father died of an aneurism when I was 16 years old, and Mike's father was killed in a routine fighter jet mission when he was still a baby.

My mother died from cancer when I was 22; I was the youngest of three children, and the only girl. I took stock of my life and made a decision—one of the best in my life in retrospect—that I needed to learn English. I knew that the best way to learn a language is to be immersed in it, so I put all my affairs in order, and without telling anyone, I applied to work as a nanny in Canada. A family sponsored me almost immediately, and that was the day my life began anew. I took the hand that life had dealt me, and chose to make the best of it, instead of passively allowing life to guide me along.

It didn't take me long to gain some fluency in English. I studied newspapers to get a sense of spelling, and watched Sesame Street with the little girl I was caring for. By the time two years had passed, my English was good enough that I was able to apply for landed immigrant status, which gave me the right to look for work in any field I desired. Of course, money was extremely tight, so while I continued to provide childcare for several families during the day, I also worked in a gas station from 6 p.m. till 1 a.m., and then ran home to sleep a few hours before running to my third job, working at a bakery. from 4 to 8 a.m. My name was on the lease for the house I shared with another nanny, so I needed to make sure that rent was paid at the end of every month. Did I feel sorry for myself as I dragged myself out of bed in the early morning after only a couple hours of sleep? I did, but I always knew that wonderful adventures were awaiting me in life. It was during this very hectic time that Mike walked into my life…literally! He walked into my room in the middle of the night, and the rest is history!

Like mine, Mike's life has always had twists and turns, and he's navigated them all without complaint. After his father died, his mother, who was pregnant with his brother, moved the family back to London, Ontario, to be near her relatives. Being raised by a single mom taught Mike a valuable skill he has used all his life: self-sufficiency. Eventually, his mother managed to save enough money, working as a bank teller, for a down payment on a small house. Getting approved for a mortgage as a single mother was no easy feat back in those days, but she managed to pull it off, and Mike has been inspired by her example ever since. We believe that hardships and obstacles are only in the way if you let them be.

So, the next time life hands you lemons, don't just make lemonade, pitch a lemonade stand and create a whole new venture for yourself! The challenges of our early lives taught Mike and I the importance of a can-do attitude, and of acting in good faith on behalf of your dreams, no matter how tempted you may be to give up. We are living testaments to the power of positive thinking, and of seeing possibilities where others only see obstacles. We also learned that sometimes the most powerful thing is acceptance of what is; you'll learn what this means when I share with you in the next section one of the greatest trials of my life.

Changing Gears

After we sold the salon, Mike and I decided it was time to start a family. By then, Mike had started his own home-based computer company, and I was enjoying helping with it. I even learned how to build computers. I enjoyed learning something new, and assembled dozens of computers at a time, lining them up in our basement in an assembly line of sorts. So, I was working, but after eight years at the salon, it was a nice change of pace. We decided that the time had come to add to our family; so, of course, we started by getting a dog.

Without informing Mike of my plans, I brought home an eight-week-old black Labrador puppy, which I had adopted from the local dog shelter. Within ten minutes of meeting him, Mike was also in love with this fluffy little bundle of joy. We named him Rambo, and called him our *firstborn*. Even Rambo says, *"Live life like someone left the gate open."*

This new *fur child* (who resembled a horse more than a dog) was wonderful, but of course, we wanted human children too. Miraculously, I became pregnant very soon after we made the decision to start trying. We were elated, but then I miscarried on the day of my first ultrasound. This was a devastating turn of events, but I was determined not to let it get me down, since I knew that it's very common to miscarry the first pregnancy. We were sad, of course, but in true Mike and Manuela style, we picked ourselves back up and tried again.

I got pregnant, again, and miscarried again.
Then again. And again and again and again.

I had six pregnancies altogether, and not one of them was viable. From the second pregnancy onward, I could only carry to twenty-two or twenty-three weeks, and then the baby's heart would stop. My medical team supported me, and we all did everything possible to keep the pregnancy, but by the sixth time, Mike and I decided it was time to call it quits. My body simply couldn't handle another evacuation operation, and I was facing my 40s. Once again, we dusted ourselves off and moved forward with our lives as best as we could.

There are no hard and fast rules that govern how we cope with grief and loss. It was devastating to give up on my dream of having children, but perhaps because I'd lost both my parents so early in life, I'd learned that if something is outside of your control, you must accept it, learn from it, and then get on with your life.

For me, it was easier to move on quickly, without over-analyzing my experience in support groups or counseling. I felt that looking forward to how we were going to re-organize our future, in light of the fact that we would not have children, was so much more uplifting than going over the *what ifs* and *if onlys*. We knew we couldn't change the past, so we re-planned our future, made a bucket list, and let Rambo be our therapist. He seemed to sense that we needed him, and he was the best silent counselor I could have asked for during that time. Since our finances were tight, our *bucket* list started as more of a *thimble* list, but we knew that giving up on our dreams altogether was not an option, and it is this attitude that has carried us to where we are today.

Live in the Now

They say that life is what happens while you're busy making other plans, but Mike and I have learned through heartache and loss that no matter what happens on your road to your goals, you must simply re-assess, re-think, and push on. It's no use looking back, because you can't change the past. Never play the victim—instead, decide to be a winner, because life truly is what you make of it.

We understand that not everyone shares our belief in moving forward from such a loss as quickly as possible. Maybe you are inclined to move more slowly because it would be too overwhelming otherwise. Perhaps you have young children depending on you, and you are afraid to give in to your grief for fear of not being able to support them in their time of need.

Healing and starting over doesn't happen in isolation, and it's very hard to do it alone. Mike and I know how fortunate we are to have each other. However, we also understand that all of us march to the beat of a different drummer.

It's important that you never lose sight of your life and your future happiness. Tragedies do not define you, but it is what you do with them that matters. Never give up on your dreams, but instead, keep marching on.

Our lives, together, have shown Mike and I, over and over again, that which does not kill us makes us stronger.

Life is What You Make It

Even as a child, I was an inquisitive little bugger who wanted to know how things worked and what the world was like beyond my front door. In fact, most of my life decisions have been based on this insatiable curiosity. I was fortunate enough to have a childhood that allowed me to see and do a lot of things that most people only dream about. Even to this day, I know many people who have never left their hometown, and I really feel that's such a waste. I say, the world is your playground—get out there and play! Sure, I could have sat in front of the TV and been a couch potato, playing video games all day long, and hanging out with the locals. We might have talked about changing the world, but it would have all gone nowhere. Instead, I chose in my youth, and I continue to choose, to venture out and see the world. I joined the Navy so I could get paid to do what I like best: travel and learn. I was born in a suitcase, so why stop now?

The author, Charlotte Vale Allen, said, *"No one is coming to your door with your life all neatly packed in suitcases for you. You must create your own life and luck."* Certainly, people love to talk about fate and luck, but it has been my experience that these things really only have a small amount of influence on your life, if any at all. Sure, some things in life are beyond your control, but why waste time worrying about what you can't change? I say, fix what you can and then move on; there are better things to do with your time.

At the end of the day, only you can decide what to make of your life—it is your choice whether to take action or let life pass you by. You can choose the latter, but don't whine and snivel at what life brings you as a result of that choice. Remember that you always get out of life what you put into it—others can't and won't do for you, and anyway, why should they? The world does not owe you anything, so you need to get over any sense of entitlement you may have. If you want something, decide what it is, make a plan, and then follow your plan to go get it. While Manuela and I are all about making the process of reaching your dreams fun and stress-free, we also know that nothing worthwhile comes without a bit of hard work and effort.

Make Every Day Count

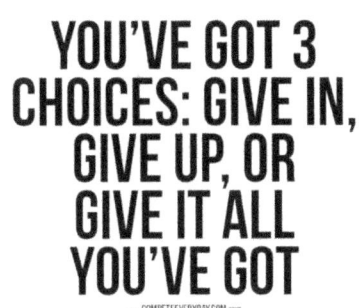

There are some who say to me that it must be nice for me to be able to do what I want in life. In response, I say to them, *"Well, why not? What is stopping you?"* Most people can't answer this question, or they have some lame excuse that justifies why they cannot reach their goals or dreams. Even worse, some people blame others for their lack of success and happiness.

We all know someone in life who is always negative and constantly spreads doom and gloom. Many times, they are friends and family, or even co-workers; they always seem to have something to complain about and are never happy. It is almost like they live to complain. Personally, I find them emotionally draining, and simply don't want to be around them. Life's too short to live this way.

If you really want to get the most out of life, surround yourself with people who inspire you, encourage you, and help you realize your potential. Decide what you want in life and do something about it. Only you, and you alone, can take action, as no one else can do it for you, and for that matter, why should they?

Don't let obstacles stand in the way of either your success or your happiness. If you set realistic expectations for what you want to accomplish, and plan accordingly, you should be able to accomplish anything you set out to do. Overcoming obstacles is often a matter of looking for alternatives, or changing your thought process. Sometimes a bit of determination is required, and perhaps talking to friends, relatives, or co-workers can help you come up with creative solutions. Always keep an open mind, and don't be afraid to take calculated risks. Nothing ventured, nothing gained.

Take responsibility for your own life, and focus on what you can do and what makes you happy. The most important aspect of taking responsibility for your life is to acknowledge that your life is your responsibility. No one can live your life for you. You are in charge. No matter how hard you try to blame others for the events of your life, each event is the result of choices you made, and are still making. Live every day as if what you do matters—because it does. Every choice you make, every action you take—matters. Your choices matter to you and create the life you live.

Share your good fortune with others. We are huge fans of paying it forward. We are also big fans of random acts of kindness. You will be pleasantly surprised at how much satisfaction it brings you. We have always said that you get out of life what you put into it—the more you put in, the more you get out—so why not?

Remember, the most valuable thing you have in life is something that once used can never be replaced: time. We only have so much time to live, so use it well.

I love it when we are meeting with other investors, and they ask Manuela, *"So, why are you guys so motivated,"* and her reply is, *"Unlike most investors, our 'best by date' is fast approaching."*

Kidnapping Out of Town Visitors

When Mike had his computer business, he was working on new product development. A friend of ours was working for a firm at the time that helped obtain grants from the government for businesses doing research and development. He was successful in getting a grant for us and, as a gesture of appreciation, we treated him and his wife to a beautiful meal. We hired a stretch limousine to take us there and back, so we could have a few drinks without having to worry about driving home.

While enjoying a fabulous meal in downtown Vancouver, there was a middle aged couple at the table beside us, also enjoying an extraordinary meal. Close to the end of the meal, we started talking to each other. They were from Texas, attending a surgeon's conference in Vancouver for a few days, and wanted to know some of the highlights of Vancouver. Instead of telling them where to go and what to see, we decided to abduct them and give them a city tour from the comfort of our spacious limo, while leisurely enjoying some drinks. Our driver knew all the right spots, and we finished the tour in Stanley Park, a park over 400 hectares, in the middle of the city, bordering the Pacific Ocean. We picked a spot to stop the car and got out to walk around and enjoy the views. The park had a sizable population of raccoons, all hefty and well fed from the park visitors. We had done this before, so prior to leaving home, we had packed some dry dog food to go feed them. They are so used to people that they came up to us and very gently took the food from our hands. The out of town couple couldn't believe their eyes, but they sure enjoyed interacting and feeding them.

We then returned our very trusting new friends to their hotel and wished them a great stay and visit for the next few days.

That couple was very brave and trusting to hop in our car and let us take them away late at night for a drive around town. Many fun and amazing memories were made that night, and we know that that couple couldn't wait to go home and tell everyone how they got kidnapped in Vancouver, to go feed raccoons in the park with complete strangers! We, too, recount that evening with smiles when we get together with our *accomplices* we had originally been out with for dinner.

Chapter 7
Happiness Starts At Home

I'm so happy here ... leave me alone.

Chapter 7
Happiness Starts At Home

"Where we love is home, home that our feet may leave, but not our hearts."
– Oliver Wendell Holmes, Jr.

I should warn you that this chapter's all me; but don't worry, Manuela will be back soon! Manuela and I know we're fortunate to live the life we do, but we also know that we've created it largely through our own efforts. We love to travel and experience new things, but we always enjoy returning to the comforts of home, and adding new souvenirs (and wine!) to our collection. Having a home is so important to us, and we know it is important to everyone. That's why, for us, investing in real estate has been a great vehicle to help us meet our financial and life goals. In our role as investors, we never forget our roots, and we work diligently to help others also create a home, and indeed a life, that brings as much joy to them as ours does to us.

Home Sweet Home

Manuela and I have shared many homes together, but when we first move in, it's nothing more than an empty space—just a house. But we work hard to make that space our home, which we never want to leave. We feel a commitment to one another and our home, turning it in to a place we are proud to call our own.

Each time we return from a vacation, no matter how far away or how long we are gone, this warm feeling, which is always present in our family home, rushes over us, and we know we are where we belong.

Remember how we talked about comfort zones in Chapter 2? Well, your home should be your ultimate comfort zone…a place so safe and inviting that it frees you from the stresses of every day mental or emotional pressures. If your home can provide that comfort, then you won't have the need for mental comfort zones, which rob you by keeping you stuck with less than you deserve.

We have found that creating a delightful home provides us with a magical comfort zone that we can always return to, no matter what adventures we've had or projects we've worked on.

We all need the security of a haven like this, because we can draw courage from it to venture on and explore new treasured destinies. When we're at home, we recharge, re-think, and then we return to ourselves. That's why we feel it's so important to make that *welcome home* feeling as powerful as we can, and all it takes is our personal touches inspired by the love we share of our home. It's a natural extension of your individuality, and you need to make sure it reflects your tastes and sensibilities.

Our custom designed front yard…Reflecting our own love for life!

We have made our home special in so many ways, and it is one of our greatest sources of pride. As an example, I have already shared with you Manuela's flare for design, creating her *jewelry wall that adorns our bathroom*. This feature reflects her love of beauty and unique gift for making our home personal.

I have done my part by working on our landscaping, as I shared in Chapter 2. It had been a new venture, but I conquered it in an effort to create a backyard oasis, where our garden matches the rest of our home, in the degree to which it reflects who we are, far more than it would have if we had called in a professional.

We love sitting there in the evenings, having a glass of wine to the sound of running water, or having brunch on a sunny weekend. Sure, it was a ton of work, but being able to make it exactly the way we wanted it was important to me. ***There's even a special dining area for our friendly furry friend, the squirrel! So, get to know your local squirrel.***

Don't be afraid to look around your house and think of ways you can put your unique stamp on your living space. Perhaps there's a collection you have that you'd like to display more prominently, or a feature you've always wanted your house to have but didn't think you could afford. I say, try doing it yourself! You may want to display your collection of teapots, baseball caps, coins, or umbrellas—whatever it is that tickles your fancy. I encourage you to follow through with your passion.

Take a course at a local college or hardware store; read books and watch videos online to learn how you can make your home more closely reflect who you are. Then, every time you walk through your door, you will *know* you are home, in a way you never have before.

Taking It a Step Further

Owning your own home provides the roof over your head, and security, but in our view, investing in property has the potential to unlock more of the life you want to live. I've always had an interest in real estate investment, though I've also made money in other ways. Stock trading can pay off as long as you understand it, do your research, are prepared to weather the ups and downs, and know when to cut your losses. And while investing in businesses can be somewhat risky, if you always do your homework, it could be a good fit for you. Over the long haul, however, I find that real estate, as an investment, always comes out on top.

My business interest in the school has done quite well over the years. My computer company did not leave me with a lot of time to consider other investments, but I did manage to purchase four revenue-producing properties, in Whistler, during those years. At that time, these properties were grossly undervalued, and were selling at about half of their original price. I did not expect to make a lot of money on rentals, so I paid cash for the properties. My short-term objective was to have a handful of properties that would at least break even, and therefore pay for themselves eventually. I also knew I could have personal use of the properties when they were not rented out, or use them to host charitable fundraisers, or to recognize and reward business associates with a weekend on the slopes. I knew their value would increase over the long term, and in the meantime, I got to enjoy all these other benefits. These properties have afforded me the ability to take up skiing at the tender age of 59, and I am even planning to try mountain biking...*I've warned my 59-year-old knees to be prepared!* In short, my investment properties are never just sitting there; they are generating value in my life, even when they're not rented out.

When I was running the computer business, a point came when I realized that I was not getting any younger, and putting in those crazy hours was starting to take too great a toll on me. Knowing it was time for a change, I started asking myself how I could create a smaller company and work fewer hours. With my other investments doing so well, I really did not need the additional income, but I still wanted to keep myself busy, but just to a lesser degree. The prospect of quitting cold turkey scared the bejesus out of me because I had seen friends and associates do this, and they were all either dead or seriously ill within two years. I'd be damned if I was going to be one of them! *I knew*

I had things to do, places to go, and people to see before I died. I had a *huge bucket list* to go through before I kicked it (the bucket that is). The question was, *how could I make more room for those things in my life?*

A year later, I had cut back so much on the computer business that I realized it was time to let both my customers and my employees move on. I made sure that both groups were supported through the transition because, after all, my reputation was still on the line, and loyalty works both ways. I had developed a fantastic team of employees, and had some customers that I knew other business owners would kill for. How many customers do you know who pay their bills straight from a quote before placing the order? So, now you see why it was so hard for me to let go, but I knew the time had come, and that I had to go with the flow of life.

Risk, then, is not just part of life. It is life. The place between your comfort zone and your dream is where life takes place. It's the high-anxiety zone, but it's also where you discover who you are.

Finding myself with more time on my hands, I happened across an ad on LinkedIn for a complimentary, two-hour seminar in real estate investing. Of course, I knew that it would mostly consist of a sales pitch for more training, but I had nothing to lose, and if nothing else, it would give me something to think about in terms of my aspiration to invest in real estate.

I knew that this could be the beginning of a new era, and I was already creating the time I needed to focus on investing. I attended the seminar, and sure enough, it led to a three-day course, but for 500 bucks, I figured the price was right. The icing on the cake was that I could bring someone of my choosing along for the ride. I didn't know if my wife, Manuela, would be interested, but I figured that if she wasn't, I could easily find a friend who would be.

I came running home from the seminar and told Manuela all about it, and was pleased to find that she was just as enthusiastic about it as I was. Needless to say, I was ecstatic at her response, and we both realized that this would be something else that we could share together. Eager to get on with the training, we flew to Calgary, because the next course in Vancouver wasn't for a few more months, and we both wanted to get started right away. The three-day course was an introduction to real estate investing, which basically just served to show us how much we had to learn. It was just the tip of the iceberg; so, of course, we signed up for even more training.

Within two days of returning home from our first real estate course, I already had my first deal put together with another investor in Ontario. The profit from just this one deal paid for all of the training we had invested in, and that's what happens when you set clear goals and take action towards them! So many people are too nervous to jump into something new because they only see the negative *what ifs*, and not the positive ones. It's been my experience that in order to be successful, you simply have to go for it. Of course, you need to do your research and be clear about what's realistic for you at the time, but stop letting irrational fear hold you back. When you do, you won't be the only one who benefits…everyone around you will too. Now, Manuela and I are experienced real estate investors; we're able to help others find their homes and create the lives they want to live, in a way that might not have seemed possible before. You deserve to have everything you want in life, but more than that, when you do, you will benefit others as well.

Any Dream Is Possible

In our culture, there is an expectation that you will grow up, buy a home, acquire a mortgage, and work hard all your life to pay off your home. This expectation is part of a deeply-ingrained set of beliefs from our society, which tells us what we should want and how we need to go after it. Of course, we all want a home to call our own. The rules that mortgage companies and banks now have allows them to shut people out, who could otherwise afford to pay a mortgage but may not qualify in other ways. That always bothered Manuela and me, because we believe that everyone who can pay for it, deserves a home of their own.

For example, take the case of a fictional couple, whom we'll call Ted and Alice. They are earning enough to pay a mortgage, but they had to pay for Alice's mom's second cousin's operation in Timbuktu (another place we recommend visiting by the way). This made Ted and Alice burn through their savings, leaving them unable to raise the down payment they needed to satisfy the mortgage company's requirements. Ted and Alice are good people, and financially sound, but they don't look good on paper to a bank. Just because of this, it seems they're doomed to keep throwing money away, renting a house that will never be theirs.

When news of their plight reached me, I thought, *"Wait a minute; what if a percentage of the rent they paid could be put toward buying their own home?"* That would transform paying rent from *money down the drain* every month into a sound investment in their future. Sure, they wouldn't be earning equity, but they would be in a better position than they had been with a traditional rental. ZuZu Properties helped Ted and Alice create this arrangement, and now they care for their rental home as if it was their own because they know they are actively working toward that goal. It was people like this that inspired us to found ZuZu Properties, as we know so many Teds and Alice's who are good people and should be able to own their own castle. To us, it seemed like a no-brainer to find a way to offer that to people.

If Ted and Alice's Uncle Marvin and Auntie Mavis are clunking around in that five-bedroom house, but the kids have all flown the coop, why should they sit on all that equity and not be venturing off on wine tours, treks across Madagascar, or taking up fencing? It's important, always, to know what you want from life, and also what you truly need. You might think you need a dining room that seats 16, but you really only use it once a year, right? Maybe what you need now is a smaller, cozier home that gives you the freedom to enjoy all the things you put off while your kids were growing up. Uncle Marvin and Auntie Mavis might just be the right couple to turn the keys over to Ted and Alice, and let them host the holiday dinner this year, while earning a rental income that covers their new mortgage on the condo and the marina fees for Marvin's new sailboat. (Marvin could even finally buy that Skipper hat he's been eyeing.) It's a win/win situation!

Why do we offer this rent-to-own service at ZuZu Properties? We believe that everyone deserves a safe and prosperous retirement, as well as a home to call their own. Interest rates on savings accounts are at record lows, yet other investments can be dangerously risky. That's why we designed our programs to provide a reliable source of safe income to investors, while providing worthy people with a home to call their own at the same time. By bringing together those who have homes for sale and the financial capacity to finance the mortgage with those who are committed to the dream of home ownership, we can help both groups achieve their financial goals…and their dreams.

Chapter 8
Living Life to the Fullest

By Far the Best Ride to Tour Any City

Chapter 8
Living Life to the Fullest

Life, On Your Own Terms

"Plunge boldly into the thick of life, and seize it where you will; it is always interesting."
– Johann Wolfgang Von Goethe

Have you noticed that everyone loves to spout their favorite advice about how to live life? *Life is what you make it; live this day like it's your last; when life hands you lemons, make lemonade;* and so on. But as tired as those lines are, you have to admit there's a lot of truth in them. Have you also noticed that the people who are quickest to hand you a quote are usually the ones who most need to listen to it? It's natural, of course, to look for solace in old chestnuts when life is giving us a hard time, but Manuela and I know the most constructive thing to do is to figure out what we want in life and go after it. Above all, never believe you must stick to one thing all your life. Each of us has had several careers, yet we still enjoy learning and reinventing ourselves at every opportunity.

Mike and I would like to share a story of a special couple, who have never allowed a wall of defeat to stand in their way, and courageously faced down life's demons and institutional demands that threw up the road blocks for achieving their dream of owning their very own home. We found their strength invigorating, and a testimony to everyone who believes they should never give up! The persistence and courage of Jennifer and Dale, to face the adversities and come out a winner, was inspirational to us and to all that know them, and we are quite honored to be their friends and be allowed to take this remarkable journey with them.

Theirs is a journey you will want to read carefully as they take you on a heart wrenching adventure but one they refused to give up.

See It, Like It, Do It

Achieving Their Dream, by Jennifer and Dale

Drum roll please………Introducing Jennifer and Dale………………
Victory smiles and reigns on Jennifer and Dale.

Jennifer and Dale Celebrating Their Dream

A friend of ours loved the story behind Jennifer and Dale, so we asked her to speak with them and write a story of their events, so it stayed impartial from our point of view!

Here it goes...

Do you believe in fairytales? Well, I do, and the story of Cinderella comes to mind when thinking about the two of them...Jennifer and Dale. They had what most of us have in life, and that's the dream of owning their own home.

Dale had never owned a property before, but Jennifer had. The two had their appetite wet for ownership and had decided it was time to move forward. Their story has many ups and downs, but they both had one path that they shared in common. They both had come from troubled home lives and knew what the world of struggle was like for anything they wanted or they had acquired in life. But they also had one important trait that is missing in some young couples with a dream... they not only had the hope of this dream, they had guts, determination, and the spirit to do anything it took to become home owners...and they became captains of their own destiny, owning their dream.

What do you need to buy anything? Money! But, it was in short supply for Jennifer and Dale. Worse yet, Jennifer, who had struggled to work hard and save a down payment, lost every part of it, but not because of a frivolous spending spree. She had stepped up to help her brother, who had several children, and a wife that had passed away, devastating the entire family. Jennifer took time off from work to aid her grieving family. The problem was that it now meant no work, so her savings became depleted and her credit was ruined. She had put her family before her lifelong dream of home ownership, and it was gone.

Did she or they give up? No; her spirit, with the help of Dale, set their dream to the side for only a while, so they could dig out from debt, pooling their funds again for that much needed down payment. Now, both *Jennifer and Dale,* are happily working at jobs they enjoy, making life what it should be! Most of us struggle at one time or another, but what made their story unique was their sheer determination to conquer their dream and not just sit back waiting for someone to come along and hand it to them.

Fate was their lucky card! They had met *Mike and Manuela Noel*, who were successful people that just happened to find life's journey far more enjoyable if they could give complete strangers a leg up in life. You may ask why, but that one is easy…they had endured many of the same struggles themselves, and had come from families where they had known what family emotional support was, and how to work hard, saving what was needed to get ahead. Jennifer had described them as compassionate people who did not judge anyone, and who swept in like the Prince in Cinderella's story. Jennifer and Dale would also soon meet the wicked stepmother and sisters, as they dealt with a few lenders that may or may not have had their best interest at heart.

Their dream came in the form of a foreclosure available at a decent price, but it also came with a lot of work. Fortunately, there was no wicked stepfamily to detour their efforts…instead, Mike and Manuela were there like cheerleaders!

From Left to Right: *Mike, Jennifer, Manuela and Dale*

Mike and Manuela had only one real requirement before extending a hand…*Can you guess what that was?* They did not care if you had money, though it would've made it easier, but they wanted to see if those they helped would step up and put in what they called *sweat equity!* You heard me right: they were interested in knowing just how much someone wanted the dream they professed to desire so badly, and what they were willing to do! Once they saw that *Jennifer and Dale* were not just talkers, they too rolled up their sleeves, and not only financially assisted them but physically did as well, painting and repairing whatever needed to be done.

But first, let's back up and tell you what they shared about their steps along the way. *Jennifer and Dale* had a couple of sad disappointments when making an offer on two other properties, with one where they had been outbid, and the other due to a problem at the bank. Determined not to quit, they pushed on, in spite of being rejected by the bank…due to the bad credit report from the time Jennifer had taken off work to help her family.

As I listened to their story, I did keep wondering if a happy ending was anywhere on their path! Here is where things became hopeful, as I listened with baited breath. Do you remember how I told you about *Mike ad Manuela* being interested in *sweat equity?* Well, they had been giving *Jennifer and Dale* homework to complete, knowing if it were to be completed on time, that they were helping a couple that wanted a dream to become a reality. *Mike and Manuela* had a plan for *rent-to-own properties*, but were so different from others who offered the same idea. They actually cared about those that crossed their paths, and the three-year program they instituted worked out for *Jennifer and Dale*, and many others.

The happy day finally arrived when they all found themselves shopping at a hardware and appliance store, for all of the interior needs that their soon-to-be home needed to have. Shopping for bargains and necessities, Jennifer and Dale were up to it all…from paint to appliances, and everything in between! In fact, Jennifer shared that it was fun shopping with another man in the appliance store, selecting what she wanted, with her husband on one side and another man on the other! But the bonus was having *the other man* paying for it all. For Jennifer, she feels as though *Mike and Manuela* are a part of her family—like an aunt and uncle—but treating them even better than their own family.

What a happy day for them all…But the story does not end there. In spite of all the *sweat equity*, it seemed that the bank's mortgage specialist dropped the ball, and they almost lost their home—and would have, had Mike not pushed the closing date out, on several occasions.

This had not been an easy task for any of the four of them, but it rocked my boat when I heard about the mortgage specialist, who was anything but helpful, and in her own deliberate way, had almost sabotaged their dreams. Still determined, they kept shopping for and repairing everything, with the end in sight and in their hearts, working 7 days a week to finish their new home, while they also knew that at any time, they could lose out.

A glimpse of a dream come true: Jennifer and Dale's first home together, with their two adorable dogs.

The stress had to have been overwhelming, but to their credit, and with the help of *Mike and Manuela*, a dream has come true. I consider myself fortunate to have met two determined people that did not just sit and whine about wanting something, but fought for its success, and whose investment has already doubled, setting their lives on a new course from where it had been only three years ago. Don't you just love a happy ending?

Final Parting words from Dale:
If *Mik*e tells you to do something…anything…
Just Do It…and Do It NOW!

Food for Thought

Life is so much more than just making a living, though of course, if you love your career, your life will be so much more enjoyable. It's also about enjoying all that life offers: from the food you eat each day, to traveling and adventuring, sharing, helping your community, and just plain having fun. We always say, go out and enjoy life to the fullest, because you just never know what great adventure might be waiting around the corner. If you still don't believe us, you might want to go back and read Chapter 1 again!

"The most beautiful things are not associated with money; they are memories and moments. If you don't celebrate those, they can pass you by." – Alek Wek

Our point in sharing our wild and crazy whims is to let you know anything is possible in life, and you can have whatever is in your hearts if you set your mind to it and are willing to work for it. As I have shared with you before, we did not always live life this way, where we could just jet set off to Paris for dinner—we know the virtue of hard work, perseverance, and struggles, as did Jennifer and Dale.

But we learned early on that we had to scramble our lives up a bit and enjoy what we could, even if to just attend cooking classes together, where we could watch a chef prepare a meal and not only get to eat it, but take the recipe home to add to our own repertoire. However you go about it, just be sure to savor life, taste new things, and find your *pièce de résistance!*

When Manuela was working three jobs, with barely enough time to eat or sleep, I'm certain she never imagined she would one day stroll the white beaches of Zanzibar and dip her toes into its crystal-clear, jade-colored sea. I couldn't have imagined it either when we first met.

However, one thing I do know is that we both always wanted more from life. We both enjoy travel, for the experience and adventure of it, not just as a vacation. If you don't step outside your comfort zone and experience the wonders of the world, you risk getting caught up in life's trivialities and losing touch with the joy of living. I find that venturing into unknown territory always does more than anything else to expand my horizons.

The Left Turn Syndrome

In our travels, and in life, we always expect the unexpected; in fact, we sometimes go out of our way to find it. As it turns out, behind every corner, behind every tree, behind every building, lies adventure and excitement, where you least expect it. On one occasion, while on vacation, traveling down the highway, we saw an obscure sign that read something about seeing the boulders. We had no idea what this was; so we thought, why don't we make a left hand turn and check it out, as who knows what we will see? We drove down this tiny little dirt road that seemed to meander on forever.

We were starting to think we were chasing a wild goose, until we finally came around the final corner, and to our amazement, we stumbled across the Moeraki Boulders. What an amazing sight, looking at these magnificent natural boulders in the middle of nowhere. They looked like giant dinosaur eggs, scattered on the beach.

Living Life to the Fullest

We had lots of time to explore and climb the boulders. That is, the ones we could, as some of them were more than 6 feet high and weighed more than 7 tons! Drop one of those on your toe and see what happens. This was definitely not on our itinerary to visit, but we are so thankful for making that left hand turn. Life is really full of surprises, so why not take advantage of what it has to offer, at every turn.

People sometimes ask us if we have kids; so, to this, we respond, "Yes, we have two: *Mike and Manuela*." For us, age is nothing more than a number; it doesn't hold us back. You can enjoy life at any age. I have to admit that as we get older, I sometimes have to pinch and say to myself, *"Whoa, I am no longer 20, so maybe leaping off tall buildings should be left to the young!"* In other words, though my mind is willing, the ole rack of bones has a totally different story. My point is, enjoy life while you have the health and stamina to take risks, and never miss the left hand turns in life.

Manuela and I have been from Istanbul to Dubai, and met ZuZu the camel, at Petra, on the way. We've traveled to New Zealand, where I got to run over a car with a T52 Centurion Tank (um, oops?). We've done wine tasting tours in Sonoma County, California, and savored a twelve-course tasting menu in New York City. We've been on safaris and have taken in the majesty of herds of giraffes against the amazing landscape of Kenya.

Let Your Hair Down

Naturally, our favorite stories to tell are the more outrageous ones, but we want to make sure you realize that fun doesn't have to cost a lot of money. Mike and I don't go gallivanting off to kiss camels and drive tanks in far-flung lands every weekend, though we could if we made up our minds that it was important to us…but so much of what we do doesn't cost a lot, because we know how to find fun everywhere. We're just always on the lookout for things to do that we've never done before.

Before Mike and I met, I had taken some basic ballroom dancing classes in Switzerland. When I met Mike, he was already taking ballroom dancing classes, so becoming his dance partner was a no-brainer. We danced together for about a year, until the hair salon put a stop to it, but we never lost our love of dancing. We've always taken the opportunity to sign up for classes periodically so that our moves don't get too rusty, and so that we keep up our *staying in step with each other* in life.

We love adventure, but we also find so much joy in the little things in life. We love Christmas. While we are hosting our annual staff party, we often share our good fortune and cheer, which tends to be contagious, and it spreads like a wild fire, engulfing everyone in the restaurant! Christmas is a time to share, so we even spread the positive energy when we send a bottle of wine to an adjoining table, or pass around any extra gifts to other patrons when we had them. I figure, Christmas is about giving, so why not? We especially like to do this for young couples who are probably on a tight budget or on a first date, because we remember those days so well ourselves. The appreciation and smiles on their faces makes it all worthwhile.

Fun can be as simple as feeding peanuts to a squirrel, brightening a stranger's day with a random act of kindness, or surprising your loved one with a funny display when they return home from a trip. Some families believe that skeletons should be kept in the closet, but I came home to a family of them, all dolled up and dressed to party (see the photo—yes, this was around Halloween!) I never know what I'll come home to, because Mike loves to keep me on my toes, and I love it! Believe me, I return the favor when he goes away. It's so much fun for me not to know what's waiting for me behind the door, on my return home from a trip.

Again, the point is that fun doesn't have to mean jetting off to Paris for dinner, or even going to the best restaurant in your home town … it's whatever makes you laugh, smile, and appreciate life! Fun is the dessert in life, and without dessert, you might as well not eat at all! Look for little ways to inject more fun into your life, and watch as the tide ripples make everything better.

Smarter Spending

Walking through the door of your home is such a special feeling, whether you're returning from a long journey or a trip to the grocery store. If you're anything like us, you've put your personal touch on the space you call home, so it reflects your unique aesthetic and preferences. When I left Switzerland to make a new life in Canada, I always knew I would find a special place of my own here. Mike had learned the value of owning one's own home from a young age, so when we met, we knew that the idea of owning a home would form a cornerstone of our relationship. We feel that our home is worth every penny we paid for it, and the cost to keep it running as well. It's the one place we can always be our true selves, a place of calm in the storm. I know it sounds sentimental, but to me, my home really is my oasis in the desert of life. But one thing (and much more) I learned early on was that *if you can't pay for it now, you can't have it!*

Perhaps what helped me most was my understanding of the importance of good credit. Even in my youth, I knew that once you have credit, you need to do everything possible to keep it. I knew that it was crucial to pay your bills on time and to not spend more than you earn. I've seen so many people fall into the *buy now, pay later* trap—by the time they actually finish paying for their purchase, they could have bought it three times over with the interest they paid. But they felt sure the deal was too good to miss, when they could have had the money if they'd just waited a few more months. Having seen these patterns play out in so many people we know, Mike and I strongly believe that personal finance should be a mandatory subject in school. We both know how fortunate we are to have earned that particular credit from the University of Life, at such a young age.

When my roommate and I moved into our first little house, we scrounged garage sales and thrift stores to get the basic furnishings required to eat, sit, and sleep in our new home. Our table was set with a mismatched collection of cutlery, cups, plates, and bowls, each one sourced from a different place. But it was all functional, and we were just grateful to have what we needed.

To this day, I still don't place any value on brands or labels. I will never purchase anything that has a ridiculous price tag, just because a famous designer's name is attached to it. Whether it's clothing or accessories, I'd rather buy ten perfectly good items whose price adds up to that of one designer piece, and get more selection for a better value.

Did you know that there are both good and bad debts?? Good debt is the one that appreciates over time. A mortgage is a good debt because real estate appreciates over time, and you build equity while paying down the debt. A car loan, on the other hand, is not a good debt, since the car depreciates as soon as you drive off the car lot. We know and understand that sometimes it is necessary to have an automobile loan, because not everyone can pay cash for a new car and be handed the keys to drive away. Automobile loans do have a reasonably low interest rate, and payments can be managed well. They are a big ticket item, but we enjoy the security of a new car, for the reliability, warranty, and general peace of mind.

Credit cards, on the other hand, are a bad debt that can quickly get you into trouble if you do not know how to manage your income, and it can easily destroy your credit. They are easy to use and very appealing, yet a means of postponing a debt load. They are also great for retail therapy when needed, but if you can't keep a zero balance at the end of each month, you're headed for trouble.

We know that sometimes emergencies do happen, and you have to exceed your spending allowance or budget, but reducing the balance as soon as possible is crucial in order to avoid very high interest rates that you are charged every month.

The worst mistake you could make is to use another credit card to pay off another card's debt, as it will or could send you spiraling into a never ending vicious circle. The interest rates are so high, they could compound and break your bank, causing bankruptcy before you know it, which in turn, could then take everything you have saved, ruining the possibilities of future loans for some time.

If you find yourself in trouble and overwhelmed by credit card debts, always pay the highest one down first. Most people don't realize, but you can also call the financial institution attached to the credit card, and inquire about debt consolidation, to see if they could reduce the interest rate and your credit limit in order to pay down your debt while you are reducing your balance, and to also avoid further charges from interest accumulation.

If you have access to a line of credit, use that to pay down your credit card debt, as the interest rate is usually a lot lower than the credit card companies. As explained earlier in the book, good credit is a hot commodity in our society, and we need it. When applying for a mortgage, the lenders look at your credit, and if the debt ratio is too high to handle, you will be denied and be considered a high risk. Many lenders also charge a much higher interest rate if you are considered a high risk.

So, the bottom line is, credit cards can be very dangerous if not managed and used in a responsible manner. If you can't afford it right now, then wait until you can. Jennifer and Dale learned this valuable lesson and achieved their dream of home ownership.

Mike and I always say that it's not about how much money you have; it's about what you do with it. There are many who seem to envy our lifestyle and want what we have, but we worked hard for it, and you can have it all, just the same as we do, if you are willing to work hard at what it takes. In fact, when we started ZuZu Properties, one of our greatest desires was to assist others realize their dreams by finding a way to have a home of their own. We both know from experience that if you want something badly enough, you can find a way to make it happen. As our title states, See It (your dream), Like It (whatever you want), Do It (make it happen)!

Chapter 9
Do it Right, the First Time Around!

To the moon Alice!

Chapter 9
Do it Right, the First Time Around!

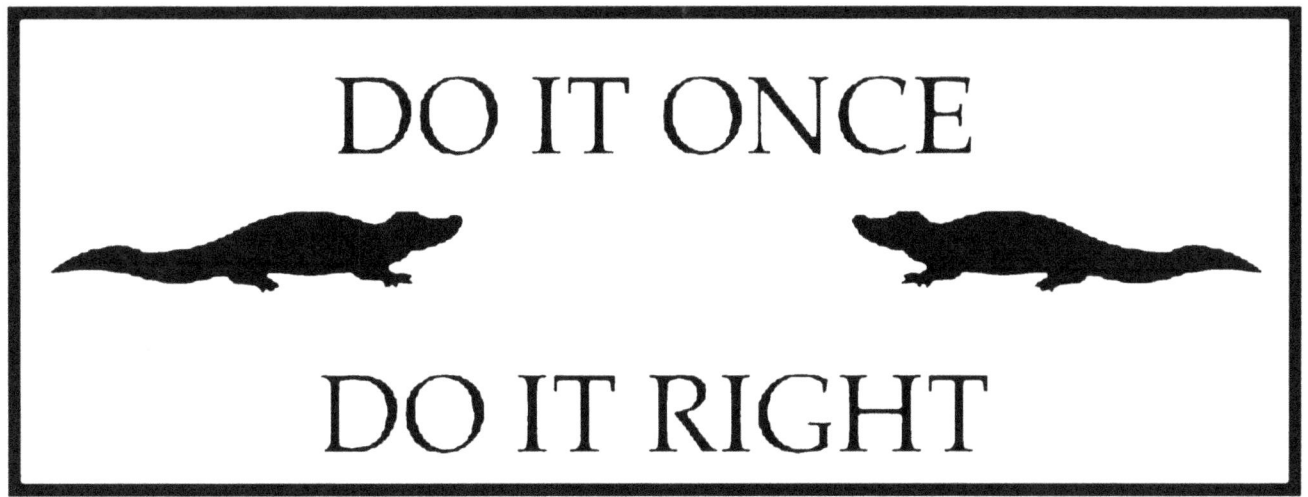

Being an entrepreneur is not for everyone, but for those who are prepared to take on the challenge, it can be one of the most rewarding experiences you can acquire. For us, it is not only about making money, which of course is why we do it in the first place, but it's also about being able to help people and provide a quality product or service. The way we look at it is, if we look after our clients, and they are happy with our service, they will spread the word. We have had so many referrals for new business from our clients, employees, and other contacts, it is unbelievable.

Being a business owner for many years, we have both learned a lot about business and investing. We have learned that things do not always go as planned, and there are always challenges along the way. If you are in the right mind set, solving problems and overcoming challenges in itself can be a rewarding experience. Yes, some problems are bigger than others, and some more challenging than others, but the biggest thing to remember is what your objectives are, and to always stay focused on the outcome. If you solve these problems and overcome your obstacles, you will have gained a valuable experience, and learned how to deal with the daily challenges of life. Next time you are faced with a similar problem, you will be better prepared to handle it. Keep in mind, the more problems you solve, the better you get at it, and the easier it becomes. While some people think being a business owner is glamorous and related to wealth, they don't realize all of the hard work that goes into being a business owner, not to mention the responsibility that goes with the territory. As much as we encourage you to take action to achieve your dreams, sometimes you need to take steps to protect yourself, which is why we wrote this chapter.

Fighting with Alligators?

It wasn't long ago that I was working with another investor who had purchased an apartment building and was having some serious challenges. The building was in a poor state of repair, tenancy was declining, and there were significant property management issues. Unfortunately, the investor was overwhelmed with problems and did not know where to start, he was bouncing around like ball in a pinball machine. To complicate matters, the investor lived offshore and had family issues to deal with as well. The investor was focused on re-organizing the bank accounts and credit cards. At one point in time, he went out and got over a dozen quotes just to repair a leaking roof, which never got repaired. He was also concerned with landscaping issues, coming up with a new company name, and a whole raft of other non-critical issues; and while they needed to be addressed at some point in time, he was not in the critical path of success. Instead, he should have stood back and realized that what was important was getting tenants back to pay the mortgage and other expenses. He did have sufficient funds to at least start renovating some of the apartments, to be able to add more tenants. The primary focus should have been on initial renovations and working with the property manager to fill what units he could. Once he improved their cash flow, and had a few bucks in the bank, then he could start working through other issues in a logical order. There is an old saying: *It is hard to remember that the original objective was to drain the swamp when you are up to your ass in alligators.*

Sometimes you just need to pull back, reassess, and come up with a new game plan. When I get really stuck trying to figure something out, I sometimes find it useful to get a good night's rest and sleep on it; you'd be surprised on what happens when you let your mind relax and come back to the problem later, usually when you least expect it. The other thing I do is talk to someone about the problem, not necessarily because they know the answer, but often I find, as I am talking and describing the problem, the solution will be right in front of my nose.

Watching Out for Your Backsides

Over the course of a year, we easily look at several hundreds of deals, and many of them do not work out for a variety of reasons. When analyzing so many deals, it is important to be able to do this quickly, so we have developed several bench marks we look at:

- Does it make financial sense?
- Can we make a profit?
- Do we have the money to do the deal?
- Do we need to get the funds from another investor or the bank?
- What are the risks?
- Consider things like target market: neighborhood; does the property fit the criteria?
- Is the investment consistent with our immediate objectives?

We like to invest in areas that have diversity in job markets. We don't like it when a specific industry has the monopoly when it comes to jobs, because if that particular industry suffers from cutbacks, or worse, that area becomes a ghost town and is unappealing to buyers and renters alike.

With experience, we have learned that sometimes you just need to trust your instincts, good or bad. We also are very diligent at not putting all our eggs in one basket and on one opportunity alone. We try to time our investments so they *mature* at different intervals, which allows us to create a steady cash flow ready to re-invest, while another investment will mature shortly after and do the same over and over. It is also very important to prepare for multiple exit strategies when examining an opportunity. If things shift slightly, or don't go as originally planned, make sure that you have at least 2 or 3 ways out of the deal. When buying a property, always expect the unexpected. Don't let your emotions take over; be prepared to walk away if things don't look quite right. Remember, you don't or won't live here, but someone else will, so it is also important not to become emotionally attached to the deal or property.

If doing a deal with partners or other investors, make sure you invest in a lawyer to make up the necessary agreements and contracts that will protect all parties involved. Long gone are the days where a handshake was a solid bond, or a scribble on a napkin, with a couple of signatures, made up a contract. Make sure that roles are clearly laid out and responsibilities assigned to all parties. Again, clearly state exit strategies and escape clauses in case something doesn't go as planned. Circumstances often can change throughout a business venture, and you have to make sure that everyone is protected. It is unfortunate that this has become so necessary, but you need to remember a paper napkin deal is fine IF everything goes as planned. If your partner objects or takes offense to having a contract, they are probably hiding something, in which case they are not someone you want to do business with, so just walk away.

Ask your business partners about their past investments, if any, or experiences. Everyone needs to bring something of value to the table and contribute to the venture. If we fast track a deal or take short cuts to make it happen sooner, it does not always work out; in fact, in some cases, it is better not to take short cuts, and, if necessary, walk away from the deal.

Watch for telltale signs of potential problems. If it's too good to be true, it probably is. My personal favorite is, *"Trust Me"*…I always run for the hills when I hear that one. If you do all the work, and your partners are dragging their butts, it is never a good sign. Listen to what they say; does it make sense? If not, check it out, because it probably is not true. This is a difficult one to gauge, and you really need to keep your eyes and ears open. **When in doubt, get out**.

Don't take anything at face value, verify what you have been told, check it out independently, and do your own research. A good example is, if someone gives me a phone number and reference, I look up the contact information myself, to make sure it is valid. It is amazing what you can do with

Google these days. Many employers are doing this, and you should too. Be sure to look someone up on Facebook, LinkedIn, and other social media channels. You will be absolutely surprised at what you can find or not find out. If you find them, and their page is completely blank, watch out; sometimes people who are hiding something don't want to be found for a variety of reasons.

If things are starting to deteriorate, make sure to keep good records, especially emails and other written correspondence. Emails are an excellent way to track and record conversations, send and receive important correspondence, and confirm meetings. This is important to do to keep everyone accountable. When responding to emails, be specific and answer all of the questions. Many people using email miss 90% of what is in them, and simply don't read the whole message. Take the time to be specific and clear.

If you are lending money for a project or a venture, be sure to protect yourself. You want that loan to be secured to something and have a distinct time line. Also you want to try to be on the title of the property you are investing in, and preferably don't go past being in the second position lender, to increase the odds of getting your money back, if forced to sell.

Watch out for someone who consistently over promises and under delivers. Unfortunately, we have had a few bad experiences with this, and it can be quite costly at the end of the day. In this case, it is important to check references and credentials.

Often, they are very personable and likable; they have perfected the art of telling you what you want to hear and are very good at it. Once they have what they want, you can be sure they will disappear, leaving you to hold the bag.

Avoid partners who want to take shortcuts to either speed things up or save money. We believe in delivering a quality product that will last for years to come. So many investors like to *put lipstick on a pig,* as we call it. The product looks like crap and falls apart very quickly. Our reputation is important to us, so being cheap is not the way to go. If you do the job correctly the first time, it is often less expensive in the long run. Things like maintenance costs actually come down as a result, saving you money in the long run.

Don't do a deal just for the sake of doing a deal; they often do not work out. We know so many investors just starting out who are looking for their first deal. Yes, your first deal is the most difficult to get, but take the time to make the best deal you can.

Sometimes, when you are talking to a new prospective partner, everything seems to run smoothly; you often share the same values and have common objectives. This can be a great way to start a new relationship; it can also lead to disappointment if you are taken advantage of. Try to find a way to shake the tree loose and see what drops out, before it is too late.

Avoid getting too caught up in the deal and missing other telltale signs of problems. Every now and then, it is important to come up for air and take stock of your surroundings. Ask yourself if what you are doing makes sense; are you on track, have the objectives changed, have the players changed, is everyone else on track and carrying their weight?

Do the opposite to the rest of the market; contrarian investing works. I have done this on several occasions with fantastic results in real estate, the stock market, and other business ventures. You need to understand your investment and what drives it, but with some carefully planned calculated risks, you too can do amazing things. Watch the investment and business cycles carefully, and make your move. Just because everyone is doing it does not mean that you have to; step out from the crowd and do it your way.

When you see an opportunity, stay on your toes and be prepared to act quickly. We have seen so many times where there is a smoking deal on the table, but everyone just sits around and looks at it without doing something about it. Any savy investor knows that if you don't take immediate action, someone else will—if you snooze, you lose.

Written quotes are worth their weight in gold. We had a situation with one of our properties that needed both house repairs and a new roof on the garage. Our property manager obtained the quotes we needed, but the one for the roof we thought was too high, so we wanted another competitive quote. As it turns out, there was a misunderstanding with the contractor, and they did both jobs contrary to our instructions. Fortunately, we had a clear email trail stating what we wanted. Just as importantly, I also signed and dated the quote for the house repairs, rejecting the garage roof. When I talked to the property manager afterwards, there was no argument, and everything was as clear as daylight. They even went on to say that even though the contractor did the roof without authorization, we did not in fact need to pay them for the work at all. The way I looked at it was that at some point in time, I would have to replace the roof; I just thought the quote was a bit on the high side. After talking to the property manager, we agreed to pay 50% of the cost. To me, this is a win, win, win situation. The contractor recovered some of his cost, we gained credibility with the property manager for being fair in our dealings, and we ended up with a super deal on the roof. *Why not*?

Don't underestimate the value of your accountant when starting any new venture, or even shifting gears for that matter. Accountants will help you maximize your investment in a variety of ways. Knowing if you should incorporate or not is a big one. Different organizational structures have different tax consequences; this is where accountants really shine and can save you a lot of money. The other consideration, when determining your organizational structure, is risk factor.

Corporations usually have better limited liability protection. Depending on the outcome of talking to your accountant, they will provide any necessary instructions to your lawyer for setting up your corporation. Whenever we start any new venture or partnership, or change strategies, we always talk to our accountant first; they are worth their weight in gold.

Your Net Worth Equals Your Network

In business, it is important to always build and develop your network. This is a constant process that should never end. When we meet people, we always let them know what we do, regardless of who they are. While this particular person may not necessarily be a match for our network, they often may know someone who is. Referrals are gold, so be sure to acknowledge and reward them.

Establish yourself with credibility. Do what you say, and say what you do. We are very up front with what we tell others, and if we make a commitment, we always follow through.

While we still look for new opportunities, now that we are established, people bring the deals to us. We always commit to at least looking behind every door and making decisions very quickly. *We don't believe in kicking the tires.* Time is important for everyone, so don't waste it. If we close on the deal, we always make sure we show our appreciation, in one form or another, to whomever brought the deal to us. By rewarding members of our network, they continue to bring us more opportunities, so it really pays off in the long run, and develops long-term relationships.

Some fantastic places to develop your network include the local Chamber of Commerce. If we are looking for a new supplier, this is the first place we look. The way we figure, if someone takes the time and makes the financial commitment to join the local chamber, they are less likely to be fly-by-nighters. In developing our network, we work closely with mortgage brokers, realtors, contractors, lawyers, and accountants, just to mention a few, which are all likely to be chamber members.

Meet as many people as you can, and let them know who you are and what you do.

Other organizations that we like to join include the local real estate investment group. They are like-minded individuals that share the same interests. They are a huge resource to share knowledge and experience with. Some people say not to talk to the competition; we say, *why not?* The fact of the matter is, that while you may keep some of your innermost secrets to yourself, there is more than enough business to go around. By talking to other investors, you may develop new partnerships where you least expect them. If you take the time to look around, you will find, even in the retail industry, there are clusters of similar types of business everywhere you look. Gas stations are the most obvious, and hair salons, clothing stores, banks, fast food restaurants, etc.…just to mention a few. The retail industry has recognized that having competition nearby is actually good for business.

While the above examples of networking are related to our real estate business, the principles are the same for any other type of business. The local chamber fits most types of business and is pretty universal. Other sources of networking can include things like the Rotary Club, meet-up groups, memberships, and other associations. Attending trade shows can help you with establishing new contacts and meeting prospective suppliers. Remember, when attending trade shows, not to monopolize their time; trade shows can be costly and are designed for them to generate new business. If you make a new contact, arrange to meet with them privately after the show has completed.

When talking to other people, we listen to what they say, and if it looks like there might be an opportunity to investigate further, we certainly will. A good example of this is when we were visiting a resort and noticed that there were quite a few businesses that had closed. Considering the resort is usually packed with tourists, this did not make a lot of sense. We started talking to the locals to find out what was happening. As it turns out, the businesses were doing quite well but could not get enough staff to keep them running, so had to close their doors. Then we started talking to the locals, and we found out that one of the biggest problems in the community was a severe lack of housing for workers. There were lots of hotels for the tourists but limited accommodation for workers. There were stories of four or five people sharing a one-bedroom condo and paying exorbitant rents. Talking to business owners, we discovered that some of them would even rent accommodations for their staff, if they could find something. This presents a huge opportunity to develop a staff housing complex, which will be our next project. If you listen, there are opportunities everywhere you go.

Chapter 10
It's The Memories That Count

TASTE OF HEAVEN

Chapter 10
It's The Memories That Count

Finding What Works In Life

Each day, for Manuela and I is like a treasure hunt. We are always looking for the next new challenge in life, be it for one another or to find someone seeking help. Pleasurable memories can happen anywhere and at any time, but responsibility comes with each passing day we decide it's time to shake up our routine.

If our only message to you could be to toss your worries out and replace them with the lighter side of life, then that is exactly what we would tell you. Yes, you do need to work hard for what you want in life, but if you do not stop to enjoy it, or step out of a comfort zone and your everyday routine, then you have missed the largest payout of life…memories! We say: *Work hard, show your strength and even your vulnerabilities (soft side), but remember to play, even harder!*

Don't be afraid to share the softer side of yourself. Manuela loves our dogs that come into our lives, and they give back so much.

Speaking about fun and living life on the edge, here's my story of sheer craziness that had us smiling in our hearts for a long time, as we experienced a life of make believe, and hopefully it will bring a smile for you as well!

See It, Like It, Do It

I know you will find this hard to believe, but this story actually happened to me earlier this year, and all in one day. I was thrown off the top of a tall building, Manuela kicked the crap out of me, and to top it all off, I got shot! WOW…what a workout! I've never been so beaten up and thoroughly exhausted. Yes, my darling wife, Manuela, who tenderly loves our dogs, made dog meat out of me! Can you imagine that?

How this all got started was when we were watching one of those *Fast and Furious* action movies, with lots of car chases and action, which is one of our favorite kinds of movies. Well, I got a bee in my bonnet and decided to use Google, searching for some crazy stunt driving, and to also discover if we could take a class. Well, I did not find stunt driving, but I did find a one-day introductory stunt school, right in our own backyard. Yes, we just had to sign up and do it, and why not? It was quite an exciting day; we were the only couple not involved in the acting community, but everyone else there were actors.

One of our instructors was none other than Arnold Schwarzenegger's stunt double. Did he have some stories for us!!! It didn't quite happen as I started the story in this paragraph, but we did learn how the rope work was done for actors leaping off of a tall building, and had the opportunity to experience it firsthand. Fortunately for us, no bones were broken trying this out.

In the afternoon, we were all paired up with a partner and were given a short story to act out based on what we learned in the morning. Our story had me playing an abusive and controlling husband, and my wife, Manuela, arriving home late. The house was a mess, and my dinner was not on the table! Well, you get the picture. You know what Manuela looks like…now, enjoy my story, and watch her turn into a single-handed vigilante!

Anyone that knows Manuela, knows this story is never going to happen in real life. Anyway, as the story goes, she comes home, and I start an argument. But she puts her dukes up and says that's enough buddy, and enough is enough! I'm not taking this crap anymore, and then she proceeds to kick the crap out of me. With a strong left hook, a jab in the old bread basket, a fast right upper cut and a knee right in the, well you know, the family jewels. Manuela did a fine job too, and the whole class applauded us for our scene. When we signed up for the class, we had the option to do a final scene where someone gets shot on stage. Well, I just had to do it. Yep, I got stage shot, with blood and all, you know, the ole ketchup everywhere scene (it's not really ketchup, but they do have special effects that make it look quite real). *What an amazing day, and lots of stories to share, with the whole thing caught on camera! Living on the edge is what we do best!*

And the Fun Is Just Beginning…

Happy…Happy Birthday, Baby! **SURPRISE!**

What's More Fun Than a Barrel of Monkeys?

Well, I'll tell you a secret. We love celebrations, and celebrating Manuela's 50th birthday was no exception. It just so happened that Manuela's 50th also occurred at the same time we were preparing for our mortgage burning party. Being the little conniver that I am, I set her up big time. *My turn for pay back!* I told her well in advance not to make any plans for her birthday weekend, because I had everything under control. We had been busy in preparation of having a mortgage burning party, but I just had to have even more fun...so I thought, *why not tease Manuela and dangle a carrot under her nose!* **Guess what?** It worked...throwing her completely off guard, for which she could only stew about for the next several months, waiting for her big day. What fun I was having now, but I admit it, I did worry for a brief time; if payback would be a b_ _ _ _ _...oops, sorry, but I can't say that word here!

We had invited all of our friends and neighbors, and it was going to be a huge celebration bash. Manuela, of course, helped with the guest list, which was important since I did not want to miss anyone special to her. What Manuela didn't know was that every time we invited someone for the mortgage burning party, I would contact them again right afterwards, and tell them, while it is a mortgage burning party, it is also Manuela's 50th birthday party, and a huge surprise! Once everyone knew it was a surprise for Manuela, they became so excited, wanting to pitch in, and I could not refuse! Besides, it made for even more drama surrounding that special day, making it even more exciting, and of course, making me feel like the sneaky devil that I am! It was so much fun, and it made me feel like Inspector Clouseau (from the movie, *Pink Panther*), with all of the secret phone calls and meetings. But I was surprised no one let the cat out of the bag, especially with so much conniving and so many people involved.

In the meantime, I organized so many of the details behind the scenes, along with the help of our closest friends, working like little beavers to help pull this off. As far as everyone was concerned, it looked like a mortgage burning party.

A huge success was pulling it off while Manuela helped with everything from the guest list to the food, and even some of the events planned for our guests. Finally, the day of the party came, after so much planning. All of the guests arrived and not a peep from anyone. At a set time, I had one of Manuela's friends ask her to show them her wall of jewelry upstairs and keep her distracted for about 10 to 15 minutes.

While Manuela was being distracted inside, I had organized the troops to completely transform the whole back yard into a birthday theme. I had birthday decorations stashed all over the backyard, and that was no easy task doing so, right under Manuela's eyes. All of my little elves knew exactly what to do when the time came. Sure enough, we got everything transformed in record time, before Manuela came outside. And when she finally did, **SURPRISE!!!** Boy, she was completely flabbergasted. *We got her big time.* And all along, little did she know, she had actually planned her own 50th birthday party! Score one for me!

Happy Birthday again, darling.

Life Has Its Rewards

Working hard and playing hard does have its rewards. Taking action to build a better life, and help others in real estate, has resulted in us being inducted into the International Investor Hall of Fame, 2017.

Our real estate investment journey for the past four years has been very rewarding in many different ways. Yes, we were able to make it financially profitable, but most of all, we were able to help so many people move toward their dream of home ownership. By lending them a hand to guide them through it, and staying with them throughout the process, it proved to be successful. Either it is a *rent-to-own* deal, or buying the ugly house on the block, and turning it into the most beautiful home on that block. Then we are able to sell it, or be helpful to other investors with funding some of their projects, while we have the best time doing it all.

When we took the real estate investment course, we also had a mentor to help us, one on one, with whatever we needed to better focus on, or to learn about different strategies that could help us further down the road. Throughout the past 4 years, we stayed in touch with our mentor, and contacted him every time we had something that required his expertise or advice, on any deal we were looking to do. Occasionally, we would meet up for a meal or coffee when he traveled to Vancouver, to catch up. He was always keen to hear the stories we had, and interested to know what we were working on next. He loved the fact that we were taking action but limiting the risks by reaching out if needed, especially if we didn't have enough experience with some facets of investing.

On one of our mentor's visits, in the spring of 2017, he had asked us for permission to submit our names in the International Hall of Fame event, coming up that following November in Orlando, Florida. We had no idea that there even was such an event, and he explained that that symposium was held every year and attended by more than 600 people. He further said that we might be a good fit for that reward, without giving us false hopes. Once again, we said…yes!

Sometime later, we received an email from the education headquarters, with the paperwork required for the selection process for the Induction into the Hall of Fame. Mike spent countless hours going through all the investments that we did, as we were required to submit supporting documentation and proof on all of them. While Mike was doing that, I was writing the stories surrounding those deals.

Later that summer, we received word that we actually made it into the nominations and were invited to attend that November in Orlando. They paid for all of the accommodations and treated us like royalty for the duration of the Symposium. The night of the actual event was magical, with a champagne reception, beautiful and delicious food, people dressed up to the nines, and a ballroom packed with about 600 people from many different parts of the world. In all, 10 recipients were selected out of hundreds that were submitted. Along with another Canadian investor, we were the first Canadians to receive this prestigious award. Following the ceremonies, we were approached by many attendees, having pictures taken with us, shaking our hands, and congratulating us for this amazing achievement. For many, it was a boost and an inspiration to be there, as we were able to inspire them to also become Hall of Famers.

The award is one thing, but we also received unlimited education for the remainder of our lives, anywhere in the world that they teach, and that is huge!

By the end of the 3-day symposium, we went to thank all those involved in the selection and nomination process. We also wanted to know what it takes to make it to the Hall of Fame. Was it the number of deals we had done? Or how big they were? We not only wanted to know for ourselves, but throughout the 3 days, people were coming up to us asking, all the time, how we did it, and we really didn't have any answers for them. So, when we did ask the Hall of Fame committee, they did say that there are variable factors to the selection, but the big one was……*the STORY!* Our story, and the story that every transaction says about us, is what got us there. The fact that we applied ourselves in making a difference in people's lives, and were not just focused on profitability and business, gave us a big reward in return, and we are forever grateful.

We, since November, have attended another Symposium, in the spring of 2018, where we met and talked to many new investors, and we are planning to attend yet another one, in November 2018. At the Hall of Fame ceremonies, we were also given Gold name tags to wear at each and every event we attend from now on. That Gold name tag tells its own story, not with just our names, but that we are *Hall of Famers!* We often are asked to join in a class and talk to new investors about our journey so far, and it's so rewarding to have them come up to us afterwards and thank us for being so inspiring, and for sharing our successes.

Looks like the story isn't over yet, and we can't wait for the next many chapters of our lives yet to come!

Waste Not!

I'm always on the lookout for something fun to do or make. We had a potted topiary tree that got *sick* and eventually died, leaving a naked stump in the middle of a large pot. I kept looking at it from a distance, trying to figure out what I could possibly do to give it a life, and not throw it away. Well, it came to me. With a pile of cedar shingles used for fire starter, and a nail gun, I made a *decoy* to protect our koi fish.

Another day, I found an old brass chandelier, and decided that too could be made into something. I stripped it of all its electrical components, spray painted it with a black matte paint, added some silver highlights, and instead of real bulbs, I filled it with small solar lights. We hung it under the pergola, where we get a beautiful soft glow in the summer evenings.

Halloween can be as big as Christmas for some. But we always try to do or create something different. For about 12 years, we lived in a neighborhood that had a lot of car traffic and not many trick or treaters on October 31st. Because we like to be different and have fun, I decided to make a witch for a decoration for the house one year. Mike found me some wood boards, where I traced out legs, arms, and hands, using my own and tracing it out. I painted them, added a garbage bag for the body, and got a wig and hat from the local dollar store. We also found the perfect little broom to add to it. We then placed our fine lady in the corner of the house, as if she just flew in and missed the house, making a face plant. We received a lot of comments about her, especially when we put the house up for sale; cars stopped, and people came and knocked at the door, asking if the witch was moving too. Apparently, every year, school carpools and others would wait until that time of the year to make a detour and drive by the house to see the witch. We had no idea what a buzz it created, until we decided to move. To this day, we still put her up every year. She is now over 20 years old, and the only thing we had to change was the dress and hat and she now has a cape. The rest is original.

Pay It Forward

Manuela and I believe it's important to share our good fortune with those who may be less fortunate. Helen Keller said, *"Alone, we can do so little, together we can do so much,"* and supporting charitable organizations is one way we like to give back. We mix it up each year; charities, such as the Heart and Stroke Foundation, the SPCA (at Rambo's insistence), the Cancer Society, local youth 111groups, and our Chamber of Commerce events, have all received donations from us. We also support a scholarship program for Kwantlen University College. Giving to others is just another facet of fun in our lives, because what could be more enjoyable than knowing you've made a difference to others lives? When we bid on items at silent auctions for charities, it's not with an eye to getting a good deal, but to help fundraise for a worthy cause. In many cases, we often bid full asking price, or on some occasions, we bid higher.

Look around your community. What organizations are there that could use your help, and are a good fit for your time, budget, and interest? Find charities that mean something to you, and then do what you can to make a difference and mean something to them.

We love meeting people just starting out in a new venture. So often, they don't know where to start, and just need a bit of guidance. We share our experiences as guest speakers, especially at real estate classes, seminars, and other public events. We have a lot of business, life, and investing experience, so it's why we want to share it with others. Our consulting services are very expensive to meet with new entrepreneurs….usually, a coffee is considered payment in full. Helping others brings joy and happiness to us, and our reward is seeing them succeed. When they succeed, we encourage them to make sure they give themselves a reward to celebrate—it doesn't need to be anything huge, but just a little something for a job well done. In some cases, we help investors with their projects. When their project is finished, we ALL get to go out and celebrate…it is an amazing feeling not to be missed by anyone.

Every day is a gift, and another leg of your journey through life. We hope that you find and follow your joy, so you can live your life to the very fullest it can be. We're doing it, so we know that it's possible for you as well.

Next time you are going somewhere, make a left turn to see what it may have to offer you, as life is full of mystery, so go for it…who knows what joy it may bring to you next.

There are lots of stories about people taking action to achieve their dreams…This is our story…What's yours?

www.ingramcontent.com/pod-product-compliance
Lightning Source LLC
Chambersburg PA
CBHW081400070526
44583CB00020B/2610